NO GREATER LOVE

NO GREATER LOVE

The True Meaning of Martyrdom

Bishop Athanasius Schneider

TAN Books
Gastonia, North Carolina

Unless otherwise noted, Scripture quotations are from the Douay-Rheims Version of the Bible.

Cover design by Julian Kwasniewski and Jordan Avery

Cover image: *The martyr of Saint Etienne. The Martyrdom of Saint Stephen*, by Pietro Da Cortona (Berrettini), 1660 (oil on canvas). © Fine Art Images / Bridgeman Images.

Library of Congress Control Number: 2025940310

ISBN: 978-1-5051-2791-1
Kindle ISBN: 978-1-5051-2793-5
ePUB ISBN: 978-1-5051-2792-8

Published in the United States by
TAN Books
PO Box 269
Gastonia, NC 28053

www.TANBooks.com

Printed in the United States of America

“The cause, not the suffering, makes the martyr.”

—St. Augustine, Sermon 328

Contents

Part III: Eminent Examples of Martyrdom

Part IV: The Fatima Message and Martyrdom

Introduction

MARTYRDOM IS AN essential part of the life of the militant Church on earth, because she was born of the sacrifice of our redeemer Jesus Christ on the Cross, and He is the "martyr," the "faithful witness" (Apoc. 1:5) of the Father, of the supernatural and eternal truth. Jesus Christ's redeeming mission on earth was preceded by martyrs: the Innocent Children of Bethlehem and St. John the Baptist. The beginning of the earthly pilgrimage of the Church was marked with the seed of the blood of the protomartyr St. Stephen. Since then, the Church has been marked by the blood of the martyrs, the imitators of Jesus Christ, the "faithful witness," and will continue to be so until the end of time. And the martyr's blood will make the life of the Church flourish by bearing new and everlasting fruit.

Pope Pius XI explained this reality in the life of the Church with these inspiring words:

> Unbelievers and enemies of the Catholic faith, blinded by presumption, may indeed constantly renew their violent attacks against the Christian name, but in wresting

> from the bosom of the militant Church those whom they put to death, they become the instruments of their martyrdom and of their heavenly glory. [No less beautiful and true are the words of St. Leo the Great:] "The religion of Christ, founded on the mystery of the Cross, cannot be destroyed by any sort of cruelty; persecutions do not weaken, they strengthen the Church. The field of the Lord is ever ripening with new harvests, while the grains shaken loose by the tempest take root and are multiplied." [*Sermo* 82]
>
> . . . We exhort you to imitate with all diligence the great virtues of these holy martyrs, and to implore for yourselves and for the Church militant their powerful protection. If not all of us are called to shed our blood for the defense of the holy laws of God, all nonetheless, [according to the expression of St. Basil,] through evangelical abnegation, through Christian mortification of their bodies, through energetic striving after virtue, "must be martyrs of desire, in order to share with the martyrs their celestial reward." [*Hom. 19: In quadraginta martyres*]. (*Sermon for the Canonization of John Fisher and Thomas More* [May 19, 1935]).

The very foundation of all martyrdom is the Divine virtue of love. St. Therese of the Child Jesus, Doctor of the Church, ardently desired to become a martyr even in her body. Yet she recognized that the Lord called her to a higher degree of martyrdom, that of love, as she explained it in her autobiography:

> Above all, I thirst for the Martyr's crown. It was the desire of my earliest days, and the desire has deepened with the years passed in the Carmel's narrow cell. But this too is folly, since I do not sigh for one torment; I need them all to slake my thirst. Like Thee, O Adorable Spouse, I would be scourged, I would be crucified! I would be flayed like St. Bartholomew, plunged into boiling oil like St. John, or, like St. Ignatius of Antioch, ground by the teeth of wild beasts into a bread worthy of God. With St. Agnes and St. Cecilia I would offer my neck to the sword of the executioner, and like Joan of Arc I would murmur the name of Jesus at the stake. My heart thrills at the thought of the frightful tortures Christians are to suffer at the time of Anti-Christ, and I long to undergo them all. Open, O Jesus, the Book of Life, in which are written the deeds of Thy Saints: all the deeds told in that book I long to have accomplished for Thee. . . . These aspirations becoming a true martyrdom, I opened, one day, the Epistles of St. Paul to seek relief in my sufferings. My eyes fell on the 12th and 13th chapters of the First Epistle to the Corinthians. . . . The Apostle then explains how all perfect gifts are nothing without Love, that Charity is the most excellent way of going surely to God. At last I had found rest. . . . Charity provided me with the key to my vocation.

> I understood that since the Church is a body composed of different members, the noblest and most important of all the organs would not be wanting. I knew that the Church has a heart, that this heart burns with love, and that it is love alone which gives life to its members. I knew that if this love were extinguished, the Apostles would no longer preach the Gospel, and the Martyrs would refuse to shed their blood. I understood that love embraces all vocations, that it is all things, and that it reaches out through all the ages, and to the uttermost limits of the earth, because it is eternal. Then, beside myself with joy, I cried out: "O Jesus, my Love, at last I have found my vocation. My vocation is love! Yes, I have found my place in the bosom of the Church, and this place, O my God, Thou hast Thyself given to me: in the heart of the Church, my Mother, I will be LOVE!" (*Story of a Soul*, chap. 11)

Let us ask the Lord for the grace to be worthy heirs of our brothers and sisters who preceded us in all ages with the palm of martyrdom. May we be strengthened in the gift of fortitude and rooted day by day ever more in the Divine virtue of love. May the Blessed Virgin Mary, the Queen of martyrs, intercede mightily for us together with the "white-robed army of martyrs" (martyrum candidatus exercitus), the ones "who are come out of great tribulation, and have washed their robes, and have made them white in the blood of the Lamb" (Apoc. 7:14).

March 29, 2024, Holy (Good) Friday
+ Athanasius Schneider, Auxiliary Bishop
of the Archdiocese of Saint Mary in Astana

Part I:

The Christian Meaning of Martyrdom

1

Christ's Death on the Cross Is the Origin of Christian Martyrdom

"MARTYRDOM" COMES FROM the Greek word for "witness." Martyrdom is the testimony one renders to Christ and His doctrine by voluntarily undergoing death or at least suffering inflicted on oneself precisely out of hatred toward Christ and His religion. It is the supreme witness given to the truth of the Faith: it means bearing witness even unto death.

In the Book of the Apocalypse, Jesus Christ reveals Himself, in His eternal glory, as "the faithful witness (*martys*)" (Apoc. 1:5), as the "martyr" par excellence. The Lord publicly declared, before His redeeming death, that He was born and came into the world for the purpose of being a witness, of bearing witness (*martyrein*) to the truth (see John 18:37). The Church, in her liturgical prayer, affirms that every martyrdom has its origin in the sacrifice of the Cross:

"Sacrificium illud offerimus, de quo martyrium sumpsit omne principium" (Secret Prayer from the Thursday after the Third Sunday of Lent). Our Lord compared His redeeming sacrifice on the Cross to the grain of wheat that falls upon the earth and dies and that, because of this death, bears much fruit (see John 12:24). In the liturgical tradition of the Church, Our Lord Jesus Christ is called "Rex et caput martyrum" (The King and the head of the martyrs).

The death of Our Lord Jesus Christ on the Cross was the greatest act of love, and it was a Divine-human act, since His human nature was undividedly and inseparably united to His Divine nature in His Divine Person (this union being called the "hypostatic union"). St. Thomas Aquinas explains the meaning of martyrdom as the expression of the perfection of love: "Of all virtuous acts martyrdom is the greatest proof of the perfection of charity: since a man's love for a thing is proved to be so much the greater, according as that which he despises for its sake is more dear to him, or that which he chooses to suffer for its sake is more odious. Martyrdom is the most perfect of human acts, as being the sign of the greatest charity" (*Summa Theologica*, II–II, q. 124, a. 3 c). Pope Pius XII taught, "The love of the most Holy Trinity is the origin of man's redemption; it overflowed into the human will of Jesus Christ and into His adorable Heart with full efficacy and led Him, under the impulse of that love, to pour forth His blood to redeem us from the captivity of sin" (*Haurietis aquas* [May 15, 1956], 89). Christ shed His precious blood and accepted the violent death on the Cross freely and with a most perfect act of love for God the Father in order thereby to redeem sinful humankind.

Holy Scripture teaches us, "In [him] we have redemption through his blood" (Eph. 1:7) and "Neither by the blood of goats, or of calves, but by his own blood, [Christ] entered once into the holies, having obtained eternal redemption" (Heb. 9:12). The salvific value of Christ's blood is explained by Pope St. Clement (+96), a disciple of the apostles: "Let us look steadfastly to the blood of Christ, and see how precious that blood is to God which, having been shed for our salvation, has set the grace of repentance before the whole world" (*1 Clem.* 7.4). St. Augustine expressed in a concise formulation the salvific value of the blood of Christ: "Christ had a blood with which He might redeem us; and to this end He received the blood, that He might shed it for us to redeem us" (*Sermo* 344.4). St. Thomas Aquinas masterfully explained the redeeming mystery of the sacrificial death of Christ on the Cross:

> By suffering out of love and obedience, Christ gave more to God than was required to compensate for the offense of the whole human race. First of all, because of the exceeding charity from which He suffered; secondly, on account of the dignity of His life which He laid

> down in atonement, for it was the life of one who was God and man; thirdly, on account of the extent of the Passion, and the greatness of the grief endured. . . . And therefore Christ's Passion was not only a sufficient but a superabundant atonement for the sins of the human race; according to 1 John 2:2: "He is the propitiation for our sins: and not for ours only, but also for those of the whole world." (*ST*, III, q. 48, a. 2 c)

St. Augustine pointed out that besides its salvific value, Christ's sacrifice on the Cross also has the power to strengthen souls in order that they may lead a life of virtue, even to the point of martyrdom: "In order therefore to profit from this participation in the sufferings of Christ, you must have charity. How to get it? Poor beggar, how to have the love of God? Do you want me to teach you? Yes, with charity, participation in the sufferings of Christ will truly make you a martyr; the martyr being the one whose charity is crowned" (*Sermo* 169.15). By shedding His precious blood on the Cross, Christ poured out from His pierced Heart the gift of Divine love, which produces holiness of life, confession of Faith, and martyrdom in His church, as Pope Pius XII affirms:

> This divine charity is the most precious gift of the Heart of Christ and of His Spirit: It is this which imparted to the Apostles and martyrs that fortitude, by the strength

of which they fought their battles like heroes till death in order to preach the truth of the Gospel and bear witness to it by the shedding of their blood; it is this which implanted in the Doctors of the Church their intense zeal for explaining and defending the Catholic faith; this nourished the virtues of the confessors, and roused them to those marvelous works useful for their own salvation and beneficial to the salvation of others both in this life and in the next; this, finally, moved the virgins to a free and joyful withdrawal from the pleasures of the senses and to the complete dedication of themselves to the love of their heavenly Spouse. (*Haurietis aquas*, 83)

2

Martyrdom as a Divine Gift

Martyrdom is first of all a Divine gift and calling that God, in the wisdom of His Divine Providence, grants to elected souls. The sinful world represents only the historical circumstances and has, therefore, a secondary and merely instrumental, exterior place in martyrdom. Here one must recall this truth, formulated by St. Augustine: "For the almighty God would not allow any evil in his works, unless in his omnipotence and goodness, as the Supreme Good, he is able to bring forth good out of evil" (*Enchiridion* 3.11). In the document *Lumen gentium* of the Second Vatican Council, we read, "By martyrdom a disciple is transformed into an image of his Master by freely accepting death for the salvation of the world—as well as his conformity to Christ in the shedding of his blood. Though few are presented such an opportunity, nevertheless all must be prepared to confess Christ before men. They must be prepared to make this profession of faith even in the midst of persecutions, which will never be lacking to the Church, in following the way of the cross" (no. 42).

The Church never condones anyone who seeks out martyrdom. One must leave any initiative to the Lord, since He gives the necessary grace of strength to endure sufferings and death for His sake. We possess a moving example in the young martyr St. Felicity, who suffered martyrdom together with St. Perpetua in 203 in Carthage, North Africa. Perpetua was a recently married noblewoman, twenty-two years old at the time of her death, and mother of an infant she was nursing. Felicity was an enslaved woman, imprisoned with her, and pregnant at the time. In the *Passion of SS. Perpetua and Felicity*, we read, "She suffered a good deal in her labor because of the natural difficulty of an eight months' delivery. Hence one of the assistants of the prison guards said to her: 'You suffer so much now—what will you do when you are tossed to the beasts? Little did you think of them when you refused to sacrifice.' 'What I am suffering now,' she replied, 'I suffer by myself. But then another will be inside me who will suffer for me, just as I shall be suffering for him.'"

We see the Divine calling and the power of Divine grace operating in the Christian martyr in a very striking manner in the martyrdom of children or adolescents, especially in the case of girls, since they are physically weaker than the male sex. In the following moving report, St. Ambrose tells us how Divine grace worked admirably in the martyrdom of the twelve-year-old Agnes:

> Today is the birthday of a virgin; let us imitate her purity. It is the birthday of a martyr; let us offer ourselves in sacrifice. It is the birthday of Saint Agnes, . . . who is said to have suffered martyrdom at the age of twelve. The cruelty that did not spare her youth shows all the more clearly the power of faith in finding one so young to bear witness to it. There was little or no room in that small body for a wound. Though she could scarcely receive the blow, she could rise above it. Girls of her age cannot bear even their parents' frowns and being pricked by a needle, weep as for a serious wound. Yet she shows no fear of the blood-stained hands of her executioners. She stands undaunted by heavy, clanking chains. She offers her whole body to be put to the sword by fierce soldiers. She is too young to know of death yet is ready to face it. Dragged against her will to the altars, she stretches out her hands to the Lord amid the flames, making the triumphant sign of Christ the victor on the altars of sacrilege. She puts her neck and hands in iron chains, but no chain can hold fast her tiny limbs.
>
> A new kind of martyrdom! Too young to be punished, yet old enough for a martyr's crown; unfitted for the contest, yet effortless in victory, she shows herself a master in valor despite the handicap of youth. As a bride she would not be hastening to join her husband

> with the same joy she shows as a virgin on her way to punishment, crowned not with flowers but with holiness of life, adorned not with braided hair but with Christ himself. Amid tears, she sheds no tears herself. The crowds marvel at her recklessness in throwing away her life untasted, as if she had already lived life to the full. All are amazed that one not yet of legal age can give her testimony to God. So, she succeeds in convincing others of her testimony about God, though her testimony in human affairs could not yet be accepted. What is beyond the power of nature, they argue, must come from its creator. (*De virginibus* 1.2)

True witness is demonstrated not in beautiful words or sublime thoughts, but in concrete deeds. Before Our Lord ascended to Heaven, He left the following precept to all of His disciples of all times: "You shall be witnesses (*martyres*) unto me in Jerusalem, and in all Judea, and Samaria, and even to the uttermost part of the earth" (Acts 1:8). To give one's life out of love and fidelity to Our Lord Jesus Christ is the most concrete and highest witness to others. The Lord said, "Greater love than this no man hath, that a man lay down his life for his friends. You are my friends, if you do the things that I command you" (John 15:13–14). All the souls who followed Christ on earth and who now as saints are crowned in the heavenly glory are appropriately called "witnesses," "*martyres*," as we read in Holy Scripture:

"We also having so great a cloud of witnesses (*martyrōn*) over our head, laying aside every weight and sin which surrounds us, let us run by patience to the fight proposed to us" (Heb. 12:1). To be a Christian means, therefore, to be a witness to Christ, if not through a bloody, physical martyrdom, yet at least through a spiritual martyrdom; namely, a life of suffering for Christ through any form of earthly disadvantage and humiliation. To be a Christian signifies bearing witness to Christ: "And you shall give testimony (*martyreite*), because you are with me from the beginning" (John 15:27).

God the Father, the Son, and the Holy Spirit are a "witness" (*martyr*), as we read in the Holy Scriptures: "The Father himself who hath sent me, hath given testimony (*memartyrēken*) of me" (John 5:37); "When the Paraclete cometh, whom I will send you from the Father, the Spirit of truth, who proceedeth from the Father, he shall give testimony (*martyrēsei*) of me" (John 15:26); "Jesus Christ, who is the faithful witness (*martys*), the first begotten of the dead, and the prince of the kings of the earth" (Apoc. 1:5). A martyr is a person who is murdered because of his faith in Christ and thereby conformed, interiorly and exteriorly, to Jesus Christ, Who is the origin, the prototype, and the most sublime image of a "martyr," of a witness, since the entire life and existence of Jesus Christ consisted in bearing witness to the truth, as we read in the Gospel: "For this was

I born, and for this came I into the world; that I should give testimony (*martyrēsō*) to the truth" (John 18:37). The traditional Catholic definition of a martyr comprises the following elements: physical death as a result of suffering; this death must be a witness of faith in Christ or of fidelity to the Commandments of God; the martyr should accept this physical suffering and death voluntarily. Those who die of disease, for the sake of natural convictions, or for heresy, or for their country in war, or who were killed in a genocide, or who die through suicide are not to be considered martyrs. An exception is found in the Holy Innocents, because they died instead of the Infant Christ and received in this way the baptism of blood. Martyrdom is the preeminent act of the theological virtue of love. The Second Vatican Council taught, "The Church . . . considers martyrdom as an exceptional gift and as the fullest proof of love" (*Lumen gentium*, 42).

3

Martyrdom of Blood as the Imitation of Christ: The "Red Martyrdom"

Our Lord said, "For he that will save his life, shall lose it: and he that shall lose his life for my sake, shall find it" (Matt. 16:25). Are we to understand that Our Lord, through these words, is subtly calling His followers to physical martyrdom, or is this only a type of spiritual death? These words of the Lord refer firstly to a spiritual death, as not all disciples of Christ are called to bloody martyrdom. However, every Christian must be ready to forego all earthly advantages rather than to lose his union with God, to lose the life of sanctifying grace. We must also consider the words that immediately follow Matthew 16:25: "For what doth it profit a man, if he gain the whole world, and suffer the loss of his own soul? Or what exchange shall a man give for his soul?" (Matt. 16:26). These words of the Lord insist upon the necessity of our readiness to resist sin to the point of martyrdom. These words can be compared to the following command of the Lord: "If thy hand scandalize thee, cut it off: it is better for thee to enter into life, maimed, than having two hands to go into hell, into unquenchable fire" (Mark 9:42). Similar are also the words in the Letter to the Hebrews: "For you have not yet resisted unto blood, striving against sin" (Heb. 12:4).

The Fathers of the Church provide several profound interpretations of these quoted words of the Lord. Origen, a third-century writer, gives the following interpretation: "If any one, who has grasped what salvation really is, wishes to procure the salvation of his own life, let this man having taken farewell of this life, and denied himself and taken up his own cross, and following Me, lose his own life to the world; for having lost it for My sake and for the sake of all My teaching, he will gain the end of loss of this kind—salvation" (*In Matt.* 16). St. Thomas Aquinas sees in the words of Christ in Matthew 16:25–26 a call to spiritual death for the sake of Christ. Yet corporal death for the sake of Christ is also included. St. Thomas Aquinas says, "Martyrs corporally imitate the Passion in a special way, but spiritual men imitate it spiritually, by spiritually dying for Christ. . . . It is natural to love the soul more than the body; hence, the wise man is the one who would prefer to suffer corporally rather than to endure a great disgrace. If then, it is so, a man ought rather to choose the salvation of his soul than the health of his body, even if he could possess the whole world. The detriment of the soul is inestimable harm" (*In Matt.* 16).

St. Thomas Aquinas also says,

> The truth of faith includes not only inward belief, but also outward profession, which is expressed not only by words, whereby one confesses the faith, but also by deeds, whereby a person shows that he has faith. . . . A person is said to be Christ's, not only through having faith in Christ, but also because he is actuated to virtuous deeds by the Spirit of Christ. . . . Hence to suffer as a Christian is not only to suffer in confession of the faith, which is done by words, but also to suffer for doing any good work . . . for Christ's sake. (*ST*, II–II, q. 124, a. 5, c and ad 1)

He also stated that "many holy martyrs . . . through zeal for the faith or brotherly love gave themselves up to martyrdom of their own accord" (*ST*, II–II, q. 124, a. 3, ad 1).

4

The Confession of Faith and Virginity: The "White Martyrdom"

One can have the spirit of martyrdom in confessing God heroically and living according to His commandments, as Clement of Alexandria, a Christian author from the beginning of the third century, said: "If the confession to God is martyrdom, each soul which has lived purely in the knowledge of God, which has obeyed the commandments, is a witness both by life and word, in whatever way it may be released from the body—shedding faith as blood along its whole life till its departure," and furthermore, "We call martyrdom perfection, not because the man comes to the end of his life as others, but because he has exhibited the perfect work of love" (*Strom.* 4.4). St. Augustine likewise said, "Let no one say: I cannot be a martyr, because there is now no persecution. Trials are never lacking. The battle and the crown are prepared. The Christian soul is tried, and, with the help of God, it conquers and wins a great victory; this it does enclosed in the body, with no one as its witness. It fights in its heart, it is crowned in its heart, but by Him who sees into the heart" (*Sermo de martyribus*). Pope St. Gregory the Great said, "Our Redeemer died out of love for us; let us learn to conquer ourselves out of love for him. If we do it perfectly, we not only escape impending punishments but are rewarded with glory in common with the martyrs. This is not a time of persecution, yet our peace also has its martyrdom, because even if we do not submit our necks to the metal sword, still we are putting to death the carnal desires in our hearts with a spiritual sword" (*In Ev.* hom. 3.4).The same pope explains further, "There are two kinds of martyrdom, one in intention and the other in intention and actuality. Therefore, we can be martyrs even though we are not slain by the sword of persecution. To die at the hands of persecutors is martyrdom that is performed in public; to bear insults, to love one's enemy, is martyrdom in the hidden depths of the heart" (*In Ev.* hom. 35.7).

When the bloody persecutions came to an end at the beginning of the fourth century, consecrated chastity and virginity were considered as a continuation or a kind of substitution of the bloody, red martyrdom, since consecrated chastity was the expression of a total surrender to the Lord through the virtue of charity, and martyrdom was the highest expression of charity, the ultimate imitation of Christ. The life of consecrated chastity or virginity was, therefore, considered as a white martyrdom, being a total expression (in soul and body) of the imitation of Christ. St. Methodius, bishop of Olympus in Asia Minor, himself a martyr (+311), left us an impressive explanation of the spiritual link between martyrdom and virginal life:

> [The Lord] announces that the order and holy choir of the virgins shall first enter in company with Him into the rest of the new dispensation, as into a bridal chamber. For they were martyrs, not as bearing the pains of the body for a little moment of time, but as enduring them through all their life, not shrinking from truly wrestling in an Olympian contest for the prize of chastity; but resisting the fierce torments of pleasures and fears and griefs, and the other evils of the iniquity of men, they first of all carry off the prize, taking their place in the higher rank of those who receive the promise. (*Symp.* 7.3)

About St. Anthony the Great, the father of the monastic life, St. Athanasius wrote, "When at last the persecution ceased, and the blessed Bishop Peter had borne his testimony, Antony departed, and again withdrew to his cell, and was there daily a martyr to his conscience, and contending in the conflicts of faith" (*Vita Antonii* 47). On the day she pronounced her religious vows, St. Therese of the Child Jesus wrote, "Jesus, let me die for You, a martyr; grant me martyrdom of soul or of body, or better still, grant me both!" (*The Story of a Soul*, chap. 8). St. Therese of the Child Jesus left us one of the deepest thoughts about the true meaning of martyrdom, which consists in the perfect love for Jesus Christ and the desire for an ultimate conformity to Him:

> To be a martyr is what I long for most of all. Martyrdom! I dreamed of it when I was young, and the dream has grown up with me in my little cell in Carmel. I am just as foolish about this because I do not desire any one kind of torture; I would be satisfied only with them all. I want to be scourged and crucified like You, my Spouse; flayed alive like St. Bartholomew; thrown into boiling oil like St. John; and ground by the teeth of wild beasts like St. Ignatius of Antioch, so that I might become bread worthy of God. Like St. Agnes and St. Cecilia, I want to offer my neck to the executioner's sword, and like Joan of Arc, murmur the name of Jesus at the burning stake. My heart thrills at the thought of the undreamed-of torments which will be the lot of Christians in the time of Anti-Christ! I want them all to be my lot! Open the Book of Life, my Jesus; see all the deeds recorded of the Saints! All these I want to perform for You! (*The Story of a Soul*, chap. 11)

Yet neither the bloody (red) nor the bloodless (white) martyrdom has any value if it is not motivated and performed by the virtue of love, as St. Therese observed: "Were this love to fail, martyrs would refuse to shed their blood" (*The Story of a Soul*, chap. 11).

5

Self-abnegation and Ascetism: The "Green Martyrdom"

ACCORDING TO THE seventh-century Irish *Cambrai Homily*, red martyrdom meant dying for the Faith, while green martyrdom implied severe asceticism. The homily states, *"Now there are three kinds of martyrdom, which are accounted as a cross to a man, to wit: white martyrdom, green and red martyrdom. White martyrdom consists in a man's abandoning everything he loves for God's sake, though he suffers fasting or labor thereat. Green martyrdom consists in this, that by means of fasting and labor he frees himself from his evil desires or suffers toil in penance and repentance."*

Christian life itself is defined as a life of witness, as Our Lord says, "You shall be witnesses (*martyres*) unto me in Jerusalem, and in all Judea, and Samaria, and even to the uttermost part of the earth" (Acts 1:8), and St. Paul taught that "all that will live godly in Christ Jesus, shall suffer persecution" (2 Tim. 3:12). The character of bearing a public witness to the Faith flows out specifically from the sacrament of Confirmation. St. Thomas Aquinas says that "all the sacraments are protestations of faith. Therefore just as he who is baptized receives the power of testifying to his faith by receiving the other sacraments; so he who is confirmed receives the power of publicly confessing his faith by words, as it were *ex officio*" (*ST*, III, q. 72, a. 5, ad 2). That all Catholics are required to live out martyrdom to some degree is taught by the Second Vatican Council: "By martyrdom a disciple is transformed into an image of his Master by freely accepting death for the salvation of the world—as well as his conformity to Christ in the shedding of his blood. Though few are presented such an opportunity, nevertheless all must be prepared to confess Christ before men. They must be prepared to make this profession of faith even in the midst of persecutions, which will never be lacking to the Church, in following the way of the cross" (*Lumen gentium*, 42). The Christian family has the vocation to be a witness in the midst of a pagan world, since "by its example and its witness it accuses the world of sin and enlightens those who seek the truth" (*Lumen gentium*, 35).

In the Baltimore Catechism, we find the following explanation about the intrinsic relationship between the sacrament of Confirmation and the duty to give public witness to the Catholic faith, which also includes fighting, through God's grace, against sin and temptations:

> Q. 686. What is meant by anointing the forehead with chrism in the form of a cross?
> A. By anointing the forehead with chrism in the form of a cross is meant that the Christian who is confirmed must openly profess and practice his faith, never be ashamed of it; and rather die than deny it.
> Q. 687. When must we openly profess and practice our religion?
> A. We must openly profess and practice our religion as often as we cannot do otherwise without violating some law of God or of His Church.
> Q. 688. Why have we good reason never to be ashamed of the Catholic faith?
> A. We have good reason never to be ashamed of the Catholic Faith because it is the Old Faith established by Christ and taught by His Apostles; it is the Faith for which countless Holy Martyrs suffered and died; it is the Faith that has brought true civilization, with all its benefits, into the world, and it is the only Faith that can truly reform and preserve public and private morals.
> Q. 689. Why does the bishop give the person he confirms a slight blow on the cheek?
> A. The bishop gives the person he confirms a slight blow on the cheek, to put him in mind that he must be ready to suffer everything, even death, for the sake of Christ.

Q. 690. Is it right to test ourselves through our imagination of what we would be willing to suffer for the sake of Christ?
A. It is not right to test ourselves through our imagination of what we would be willing to suffer for the sake of Christ, for such tests may lead us into sin. When a real test comes, we are assured God will give to us, as He did to the Holy Martyrs, sufficient grace to endure it.

In his study of early Church persecution, published during the Nazi era, Erik Peterson, a German philosopher and convert, explains how the imitation of Christ in the spiritual and ascetic life of a Christian is a kind of martyrdom:

> In whatever sense it may be, we can, or rather we must all accompany the Lord in his passion; and this is why the cross is not a symbol only for martyrs, it is also a symbol in general for all Christian life. It is therefore not due to an accidental historical development, as Protestant historians continue to believe, it is rather due to the very nature of things that the saints, who went through all the mortifications and all the suffering, were compared to martyrs. And although we become neither saints nor martyrs, yet we must all embrace some form of asceticism. At the bottom of Christian asceticism, there is for all of us, who, to speak with Saint Paul, try to carry the mortification of Christ in our body

> (2 Cor. 4:10) only one principle: namely the principle of compassion with Christ, of mortification with Him who, for us, was put to death. He who said: My Father, if it is possible, let this chalice depart from me (Matt. 26:39), He knows our fear, our anguish in the face of suffering and in the face of death. He knows that we tremble at having to imitate him; that we are weak, and that we do not want to take the cross upon ourselves; that we are afraid of poverty, of slander, of dishonor, of beatings, of death. But by bearing our fearful flesh, He has, in the words of Saint Athanasius, through His apparent fear, delivered us from our fear. Indeed, everything that is accomplished in the Church is accomplished in the certainty that if Christ died, he was also resurrected: so that with the suffering of Christ, it is the virtue of his resurrection which is communicated to the Church. We are baptized into the death of Christ, but we receive the Holy Spirit in baptism. And this is why the ascetic and spiritual life of Christians is not only a mortification, but also and at the same time a victory, a vivification, a transformation in the Holy Spirit. (*Zeuge der Wahrheit [Witness to the Truth]* [Leipzig: 1937], pp. 26–27)

We might now wonder why the Lord preserved Saint Mary Magdalen from martyrdom. In her case, one may assume that the interior fire of the extraordinary intensity of her repentance was considered in the eyes of God as equal to the pains of a violent physical death as a martyr. St. Mary Magdalen spent her life in a continuous repentance that was moved and sustained by a burning love. St. Cyprian of Carthage (+258) said,

> We have begun gladly to seek martyrdom while we are learning not to fear death. These are trying exercises for us, not deaths; they give to the mind the glory of fortitude; by contempt of death, they prepare for the crown.
>
> But perhaps someone may object and say, "Now in the present mortality this is a source of sorrow to me that I who had been prepared for confession and had dedicated myself with my whole heart and with all my courage to the endurance of suffering, am deprived of my martyrdom, since I am being forestalled by death." In the first place, martyrdom is not in your power, but in the giving of God, and you cannot say that you have lost what you do not know whether you deserved to receive. Then, secondly, God is a searcher of the reins and heart and the observer and judge of hidden things; He sees and praises and approves of you. And He who perceives your ready virtue will give a reward for virtue. . . . God does not ask for our blood but our faith; for neither Abraham nor Isaac nor Jacob was put to death, but, nevertheless, honored for the merits of their faith and righteousness, they have deserved to be first among

> the patriarchs, and to their feast is gathered whosoever is found faithful and just and praiseworthy. (*De mortalitate*, 16–17)

The continuous penitential life of this holy woman was an exercise in all virtues, since penance is an interior disposition accompanied by corresponding acts, including the practice of both the theological and the moral (cardinal) virtues, as St. Thomas Aquinas explains:

> Although penance is directly a species of justice, yet, in a fashion, it comprises things pertaining to all the virtues; for inasmuch as there is a justice of man towards God, it must have a share in matter pertaining to the theological virtues, the object of which is God. Consequently penance comprises faith in Christ's Passion, whereby we are cleansed of our sins, hope for pardon, and hatred of vice, which pertains to charity. Inasmuch as it is a moral virtue, it has a share of prudence, which directs all the moral virtues: but from the very nature of justice, it has not only something belonging to justice, but also something belonging to temperance and fortitude, inasmuch as those things which cause pleasure, and which pertain to temperance, and those which cause terror, which fortitude moderates, are objects of commutative justice. Accordingly it belongs to justice both to abstain from pleasure, which belongs to temperance, and to bear with

> hardships, which belongs to fortitude. (*ST*, III, q. 85, a. 3, ad 4)

In the time of the martyrs, when the Church suffered a bloody persecution, St. Cyprian praised the life of an authentic repentance and penance, for which God will grant the crown of glory:

> If any one move [God] still more by his own atonement, if he appease His anger, if he appease the wrath of an indignant God by righteous entreaty, He gives arms again whereby the vanquished may be armed; He restores and confirms the strength whereby the refreshed faith may be invigorated. The soldier will seek his contest anew; he will repeat the fight, he will provoke the enemy, and indeed by his very suffering he is made braver for the battle. He who has thus made atonement to God; he who by repentance for his deed, who by shame for his sin, has conceived more both of virtue and of faith from the very grief of his fall, heard and aided by the Lord, shall make the Church which he had lately saddened glad, and shall now deserve of the Lord not only pardon, but a crown. (*De lapsis* 36)

St. Ambrose taught that an authentic Christian life requires an invisible, interior martyrdom:

> Not only are these persecutors who are seen, but also those who are not seen, and many more persecutors,

like one persecuting king who sent orders of persecution to many, and there were different persecutors in each city or province. So too the devil directs many of his servants, not only outwardly, but also inwardly he lets them persecute the minds of individuals. It was said of these persecutions: "All who want to live devoutly in Christ will suffer persecution" (2 Tim. 3:12), "everyone," he said, he excepts no one. For who can be saved, when the Lord himself endured the trials of the persecutions? Avarice persecutes, ambition persecutes, lust persecutes, pride persecutes, fornication persecutes. Whence also the Apostle says: "Flee from fornication" (1 Cor. 6:18). For what reason would you flee if she did not pursue you? For it is the evil spirit of fornication, it is the evil spirit of covetousness, the evil spirit of pride. These are the great persecutors, who often destroy the mind of a man without the terror of a sword. Who conquer the hearts of the faithful by temptations rather than by terrors. These are your enemies to guard against, these are greater tyrants, by whom Adam was captured. Many who were crowned in public persecution, fell in secret by this persecution. He says that "outside is fighting, inside is fear" (2 Cor. 7:5), saying how great is the struggle that is within man, so that he himself would engage with him. Will he fight with his desires? The Apostle himself wavers, clings, is bound, he claims to be captive to the law of sin and death, to be overcome by the body, and not able to escape, unless he had been delivered by the grace of the Lord Jesus. Indeed, as many persecutions, so many martyrdoms. Every day you are a witness of Christ. You were tempted by the spirit of fornication, but fearing Christ's future judgment, you did not defile the chastity of mind and body: you are a martyr of Christ. You were tempted by the spirit of covetousness to encroach upon the possessions of a minor, to disregard the rights of defenseless widows, and yet by contemplation of the help of heavenly precepts you judged the wrong to be done rather than inflicted it: you are a witness of Christ. Finally, Christ wants to help such witnesses, according to what is written: "Judge the orphan and justify the widow and let us argue with the truth" (Is. 1:17), says the Lord. You were tempted by the spirit of pride, but when you saw the poor and the needy you were compassionate with a pious mind: you loved humility more than arrogance: you are a witness of Christ! What is more, you have given evidence not only of speech, but also of work. For who is a richer witness than he who confesses that the Lord Jesus came in the flesh, when he keeps the precepts of the gospel? For he that heareth and doeth not, denies Christ. Although he admits the word, he denies the works. How many said: "Lord, Lord, did we not prophesy in your name and cast out devils and do many virtues? on that day he will answer: depart from me all workers of iniquity!" (Matt. 7:22). He is the witness, who testifies to the precepts of the Lord Jesus by the deeds he has ordained. How many, then, are every day in secret the martyrs of Christ and confess Jesus as Lord! The apostle knew this martyrdom and faithful testimony of Christ, who said: "For this is our glory and the testimony of our conscience" (2 Cor. 1:12). How many were they who confessed outwardly and inwardly denied! (*In Ps. 118*, 45–48)

6

Martyrdom and the Life of the Church

ALREADY DURING THE first Christian centuries, Tertullian left us the following famous affirmation: "The blood of martyrs is the seed of new Christians" (*Apol.* 50). Since the beginning of the Church, the martyrdom of Christians has been understood as possessing a spiritual fecundity because of its connection to the death of Christ. The concept of martyrdom is, therefore, essential to the definition of the Church on earth, the militant Church. Blessed Cardinal Stepan Wyszyński (1901–1981) made in his prison notes this astonishing assertion: "The eighth sacrament in the life of the Church is martyrdom" (*A Freedom Within: The Prison Notes of Cardinal Stefan Wyszyński* [New York: 1983], p. 75). Cardinal Charles Journet also said, "If the life of Christ culminates, as at its highest point, in the testimony that he wanted to give to the truth by dying on the cross, it is clear that charity which flows out from the sacraments, will secretly push the Church to also give such a testimony at the price of her blood, in other words it will incline her towards martyrdom" (*Théologie de l'Eglise*, 2nd ed., [Paris: 1987], p. 215).

Erik Peterson wrote,

> The martyr suffers with Christ as a member of the Mystical Body. To say that the martyr suffers with Christ is to say that his passion is more than just the fact of suffering for Christ. Many soldiers died for their king; but the death of the martyr differs from that of the soldier: not only does he suffer for Jesus, it is through the death of Christ that he is led to his own death. The passion which leads Christ to death, since he is the Son of man, the incarnate God, operates in the whole Church as in His mystical body. What is important to remember is that the possibility of martyrdom, which is true in all of us, has its root in the very reality of the baptism of death of Jesus, into which we were baptized by baptism of water. We are all, says Saint Paul, baptized into the death of Christ (Rom. 6:3). What is still important to remember is that the possibility we face of having to offer our body and blood for Christ is based on the fact that the body and blood of the Lord, in which we participate, are presented to us in his chalice at Gethsemane. Baptism with water and baptism with blood therefore come from the same Lord, and they are prefigured, as Saint Cyril of Jerusalem said, by the blood and

> water that came out from the side of Jesus. (*Zeuge der Wahrheit* [Leipzig: 1937], pp. 24–25)

"Water baptism and after it, the Eucharist operate in each Christian a disposition to suffer and die with Christ: they create in him a deputation to baptism of blood, if not as to their most frequent effect, of less like their most normal effect. 'Above all, I would like to shed my blood for you, O my Beloved Lord.' It is the cry of the saint of Lisieux" (Journet, *Théologie de l'Eglise*, p. 215).

The imitation of Christ and the participation in His sacrifice of the Cross is the very motive and cause of Christian martyrdom. St. Augustine said, "The punishment does not make the martyr, but the cause does" (*Serm*o 327.1; Christi martyrem non facit poena, sed causa). In the *Letter to Diognetus* from the end of the second century, we can read how the first Christians understood their vocation in the midst of a pagan world. They believed that the persecution and the suffering they endured were spiritually fruitful:

> [Christians] love all men, but all men persecute them. Condemned because they are not understood, they are put to death but raised to life again. They live in poverty, but enrich many; they are totally destitute, but possess an abundance of everything. They suffer dishonour, but that is their glory. They are defamed but vindicated. A blessing is their answer to abuse, deference their response to insult. For the good they do they receive the

punishment of malefactors, but even then, they rejoice, as though receiving the gift of life. They are attacked by the Jews as aliens, they are persecuted by the Greeks, yet no one can explain the reason for this hatred.

To speak in general terms, we may say that the Christian is to the world what the soul is to the body. As the soul is present in every part of the body, while remaining distinct from it, so Christians are found in all the cities of the world but cannot be identified with the world. As the visible body contains the invisible soul, so Christians are seen living in the world, but their religious life remains unseen. The body hates the soul and wars against it, not because of any injury the soul has done it, but because of the restriction the soul places on its pleasures. Similarly, the world hates the Christians, not because they have done it any wrong, but because they are opposed to its enjoyments. Christians love those who hate them just as the soul loves the body and all its members despite the body's hatred. It is by the soul, enclosed within the body, that the body is held together, and similarly, it is by the Christians, detained in the world as in a prison, that the world is held together. The soul, though immortal, has a mortal dwelling place; and Christians also live for a time amidst perishable things, while awaiting the freedom from change and decay that will be theirs in heaven. As the soul benefits from the deprivation of food and drink, so Christians flourish under persecution. Such is the Christian's lofty

> and divinely appointed function, from which he is not permitted to excuse himself. (*Diogn.* 5–6)

The famous Franco-English Catholic poet and apologist Hilaire Belloc (+1953) made the following apt and prophetic observation: "If I be asked what sign we may look for to show that the advance of the Faith is at hand, I would answer by a word the modern world has forgotten: Persecution. When that shall once more be at work it will be morning" (*Survivals and New Arrivals: The Old and New Enemies of the Catholic Church* [London: 1929]). Pope St. Leo the Great (+461) spoke the following encouraging words, valid for all ages: "The religion of Christ, founded on the mystery of the Cross, cannot be destroyed by any sort of cruelty; persecutions do not weaken, they strengthen the Church. The field of the Lord is ever ripening with new harvests, while the grains shaken loose by the tempest take root and are multiplied" (*Sermo* 82.6).

The official list of the canonized saints is called with the appropriate name *Martyrologium*. The martyrs were the first saints whom the Church liturgically venerated, after the Blessed Virgin Mary and the apostles. Yet all the apostles were martyrs. Even St. John the Evangelist suffered, according to the reliable tradition of the Church, a physical martyrdom in being thrown into boiling oil in Rome, but by Divine intervention he came out unharmed. For more than a millennium, there was a feast that commemorated the martyrdom of St. John the Apostle (it was called the Feast of St. John before the Latin Gate, celebrated on May 6). The Church even had a feast (on August 1) of Old Testament martyrs, the Maccabean martyrs; that is, the mother with her seven sons (see 2 Mach. 7).

Christian martyrdom contains seven important virtues: fortitude, humility, faith, obedience, detachment, hope, and above all, charity. St. John Chrysostom (+407), himself not physically a martyr, demonstrated nonetheless in his life all the virtues of a martyr, as we can see in these deeply moving words from his last homily before his exile:

> The waters have risen and severe storms are upon us, but we do not fear drowning, for we stand firmly upon a rock. Let the sea rage, it cannot break the rock. Let the waves rise, they cannot sink the boat of Jesus. What are we to fear? Death? Life to me means Christ, and death is gain. Exile? "The earth and its fullness belong to the Lord" (Psalm 23). The confiscation of goods? We brought nothing into this world, and we shall surely take nothing from it. I have only contempt for the world's threats, I find its blessings laughable. I have no fear of poverty, no desire for wealth. I am not afraid of death nor do I long to live, except for your good. (*Hom. ante exilium* 1)

Indeed, martyrdom has always been an essential aspect of the life of the Church. Daily resounded in the Church since the first centuries are these words of her Divine Office: "Precious in the sight of the Lord is the death of his saints" (Ps. 115:15).

7 The Martyrdom of Non-Catholics

THOSE NON-CATHOLICS WHO lost their lives rather than apostatize from the Christian faith were heroes. However, one cannot call them martyrs in the same sense as the Catholic Church venerates her martyrs. In accordance with the Church's tradition, Popes Pius IX and Pius XII recognized that a person in a situation of invincible ignorance regarding the Catholic Church, but who, with the help of grace, follows the natural law, fulfilling God's commandments and believing in a just God Who rewards the good and punishes the bad, has faith by desire (*in voto*) and is somehow connected to the sole Church of Christ. Thus, that person can be saved through the Church (see Sacred Congregation of the Holy Office, Letter to the Archbishop of Boston [August 8, 1949]). Pope Benedict XIV (1740–1758), in his work *De servorum Dei beatificatione et de beatorum canonizatione*, spoke of people outside the visible Church through no fault of their own, because of invincible ignorance, who nevertheless give their lives in witness to a Catholic truth. Can they be considered martyrs? In response, Pope Benedict XIV makes an important distinction: they may have been true martyrs, but only before God, not before the Church. They would be martyrs before God, provided they were habitually willing to believe whatever the Church proposed if they had had the means to know it and their ignorance was not due to their fault. They would not be martyrs officially recognized and proclaimed by the Church because only God knows the internal dispositions of a person's soul at the hour of death. Now the Church can only make a pronouncement about external actions that can be known by one's senses. Thus, she cannot publicly consider martyrdom something that only God can know—namely, that a person in the state of invincible ignorance decided in his heart, even if only as a desire, to belong to the Catholic Church and died united to her.

The Divine truth of the uniqueness of the Church excludes any ambiguous actions, such as the canonization of non-Catholics who died as martyrs for the sake of Christ.

> "It is so evident from the clear and frequent testimonies of Holy Writ that the true Church of Jesus Christ is one, that no Christian can dare to deny it. . . .
>
> . . . Jesus Christ did not, in point of fact, institute a Church to embrace several communities similar in

nature, but in themselves distinct, and lacking those bonds which render the Church unique and indivisible after that manner in which in the symbol of our faith we profess: "I believe in one Church."

"The Church in respect of its unity belongs to the category of things indivisible by nature, though heretics try to divide it into many parts. . . . We say, therefore, that the Catholic Church is unique in its essence, in its doctrine, in its origin, and in its excellence. . . . Furthermore, the eminence of the Church arises from its unity, as the principle of its constitution—a unity surpassing all else, and having nothing like unto it or equal to it" (St. Clement of Alexandria, *Stromatum* 8.17). For this reason Christ, speaking of the mystical edifice, mentions only one Church, which he calls His own: "I will build my church"; any other Church except this one, since it has not been founded by Christ, cannot be the true Church. (Pope Leo XIII, *Satis cognitum* [June 29, 1896], 4)

8

The Heavenly Glory of the Martyrs

In the Apocalypse of St. John, also known as the Book of Revelation, the Evangelist sees a throng of 144,000 people in Heaven waving their palm branches before the throne of God. When he inquired who they were, the Evangelist was told, "These are they who are come out of great tribulation, and have washed their robes, and have made them white in the blood of the Lamb" (Apoc. 7:14). The glory in heaven, or the perfection of the beatific vision of God, will have different degrees. Our Lord said, "In my Father's house there are many mansions" (John 14:2). The degree of the eternal glory will depend on the perfection of charity, as St. Thomas Aquinas explains:

> In the first way [proximately] the mansions are distinguished according to the charity of heaven, which the more perfect it will be in anyone, the more will it render him capable of the Divine clarity, on the increase

> of which will depend the increase in perfection of the Divine vision. In the second way [remotely] the mansions are distinguished according to the charity of the way. For our actions are meritorious, not by the very substance of the action, but only by the habit of virtue with which they are informed. Now every virtue obtains its meritorious efficacy from charity, which has the end itself for its object. Hence the diversity of merit is all traced to the diversity of charity, and thus the charity of the way will distinguish the mansions by way of merit. (*ST*, Suppl., q. 93, a. 3 c)

Our Lord said, "Greater love than this no man hath, that a man lay down his life for his friends" (John 15:13).

Martyrdom finds its highest and most perfect expression in the Divine virtue of love. Our Lord Jesus Christ is the highest example, the prototype of the martyrs. All His life on earth was directed towards His bloody sacrifice on the Cross, which He desired: "I am come to cast fire on the earth: and what will I, but that it be kindled? And I have a baptism wherewith I am to be baptized: And how am I straitened until it be accomplished?" (Luke 12:49–50). In the heavenly glory, the martyrs will be following Him most closely, since the Lord surrounded Himself in His first coming here on earth with the martyrs, the Innocent Children, and after His Ascension into heaven, He gave to the young Church her first saint and martyr in St. Stephen.

Part II

Personal Relationship with Persecuted Christians and Martyrs

1

Bl. Oleksiy Zaritskiy (1912–1963)

As a child, living in the Soviet Union, I had, through my parents, an indirect contact with a martyr priest, Blessed Oleksiy Zaritskiy. He was a Ukrainian Greek-Catholic priest from the archdiocese of Lviv. He had been for several years the confessor of my parents in the underground church in the Ural Mountains, during the years 1950–1960. He baptized my elder siblings and blessed me when I was lying in the cradle (before his arrival I had already been baptized by my mother and later additionally by an underground Lithuanian Jesuit priest). Blessed Fr. Oleksiy suffered horribly in several Communist prisons and Gulags in Siberia merely for refusing to deny his Catholic faith, since he was asked to join the Russian Orthodox Church. The Communist authorities released him several years after the death of Stalin, when the severity of the persecution had receded a little bit. However, he was treated by the authorities as a persona non grata. For instance, he was refused a residence permit several times in various places. He was forced to live for a time as a homeless person. The Catholics, who loved him so much, lovingly named him "the vagabond of God." Yet in the midst of all this discrimination and these difficulties, Bl. Fr. Oleksiy developed an intense and heroic apostolate in the underground church, being aware that, at any moment, the Communist authorities could arrest and later kill him. He died in 1963 in a Gulag near Karaganda in Kazakhstan because of the bad conditions in the prison. He was beatified in 2001 as a martyr together with other Ukrainian martyrs. My parents spoke of him very frequently and told me that they had never met in their whole lives a holier priest than Fr. Oleksiy.

What impressed my parents so greatly was the heroic apostolic zeal of Bl. Oleksiy Zaritskiy. In the exteriorly dangerous and uncomfortable circumstances of the underground church, in little rooms with no windows, at times in a suffocating atmosphere, he spent whole nights hearing confessions. He celebrated with exactness and devotion the Holy Mass in Latin, in the Roman Rite (though he was a Greek-Catholic priest of the Byzantine Rite). He preached the fundamental truths of the Catholic faith. He often repeated these words: "Let us keep faithfully the Faith of our forefathers." Precious are the following quotations from the letters of Bl. Oleksiy, revealing to us his deep faith and solid spirituality regarding the Christian life: "While you live, you must not give too much importance to successes, nor despair in times of trial and misfortune. The stable faith in God should be the light that illuminates our path in life, and the fear of God will lead us to the highest wisdom. Those who live according to this law will never make mistakes and in the most difficult moments of their lives they will be able to keep their peace of soul, the peace that the world is never able to offer" (Letter from 30 August 1957). Concerning married and family life, Bl. Oleksiy gave us the following inspiring instructions:

> There is no better life than that in which you live in a good family, in which you take care of and help one another. There is no better friendship than between husband and wife. However, only those can feel happy in marriage who understand their family life in the light of the Gospel. Life is a duty! Living means glorifying the Creator through prayer. Living means doing good to others, being obedient, patient, knowing how to forgive, controlling every word that comes out of one's mouth and one's thoughts, so that they may contribute to the good of others. And the family itself is that place where one can conquer these virtues, and this for the dignity of one's soul and for the achievement of happiness already in this world. Married life is the life of incessant yielding, of perpetual sacrifice and mutual help

> between spouses in the name of God and for the common good. May this be among you! Seek God, and your soul will be alive, this is what Jesus the Saviour teaches us. Whoever does not have God in his soul, even if he had all the riches of the world, would be of no use to himself. This is that strong thought that has enlightened me until now and I am happy to consider it the highest of my life. (Letter from 13 May 1957)

Bl. Oleksiy Zaritskiy addressed the last letter of his life to his father. In it, he expresses his sincere filial love for his father and an authentic supernatural vision of the Christian life centered on the Divine Wisdom of the Cross:

> Dearest father! You are my greatest and most generous benefactor in the whole world. For 17 long years you enabled me to receive an education, you even limited yourself in sustenance so that I could do so, and now I am unable to thank you worthily. How I would like to be close to you to help you in your weakness! I sympathize with you in all this, and I carry with you this cross that Divine Providence has destined for you. I have begged for the gift of Divine Wisdom, which is the wisdom of the Cross: to endure everything patiently and consciously in order to attain eternal life. This means every day, indeed every minute, consecrating everything to the suffering Jesus, who carried His cross to Golgotha, so that we become aware of the sufferings amid

which we too must stand firm and steadfast in the hope of attaining eternal life. For it is worthwhile to sacrifice oneself absolutely, without any reservations. It is once again necessary to recall these words that I read to you in 1961 about a nun who in her apparition after death said: "Were a person while living here on earth able to see God for just a brief instant, his soul would be filled with such joy, that he would be ready to endure all the tortures and sufferings, even the cruelest in the world, in order to be able to see God once again, even for another very brief instant, even while knowing well that this is no longer possible in this life." May this thought be a comfort to you in your illness. May your strength be doubled to endure all this with the love of Jesus in the name of eternal life. (Letter from 3 October 1963)

2

Fr. Janis Pavlovskis OFMCap (1914-2000)

Another confessor of the Faith with whom I had contact was Fr. Janis Pavlovskis, a Latvian Capuchin priest who, during the time of Communism, was also persecuted and imprisoned. He died in 2000 in Riga. In 1950, he was imprisoned in one of the Soviet Gulags, in the "Karlag" (in Kazakhstan), because of the Catholic faith and the priesthood. I had known him for four years in my childhood, when my family lived in Estonia. He was my parish priest in Tartu (Estonia), he heard my first Confession, gave me First Holy Communion and the sacrament of Confirmation. In 1977, Fr. Pavlovskis went to Kazakhstan and built a chapel there, and took care of the Catholics in the city of Taras in southern Kazakhstan. In 1991, he went to Riga, in Latvia, and was the parish priest at the Church of St. Albert. Fr. Pavlovskis impressed me as a child so much that I wondered how one could become a priest. One day, after the Mass Fr. Pavlovskis celebrated, we were walking to his house, and I had the idea to ask my mother how one becomes a priest. Then my mother stopped and said to me, "In order to become a priest, it is necessary that God calls." She said nothing more. These words remain so fresh in my memory. In fact, in 2016, I was in Tartu and went to the exact spot where I asked my mother how one can become a priest. Then I celebrated Holy Mass in that church, at the high altar, where I had received my First Holy Communion from the hands of this confessor priest.

A distinguishing trait of Fr. Pavlovskis was his deep and awe-inspiring veneration for the Blessed Sacrament. Simply seeing him genuflect before the Blessed Sacrament was a moving testimony of deep faith. When we settled in Germany, I was twelve and a half years old. Just before we left for Germany, Fr. Pavlovskis blessed us, and then he said to us these words, which I will never forget: "When you go to Germany, be careful. There are some churches where Communion is given in the hand." When we heard this, we looked at one another, and my mother and father said spontaneously, "Horrible!" Really, we could not imagine how the Holy of Holies, the Living God, could be taken in the hand. That was for me utterly inconceivable. He said to us, "Please, don't go to these churches." And we promised to do as he instructed.

Fr. Pavlovskis inspired me and my siblings with veneration for the martyrs. He often spoke to us about the martyrs of the ancient Church and the persecution of the Christians. This holy priest once showed to me and my siblings a book. There was a picture of the catacombs. I asked him, "What is this?" "They are the catacombs," he responded. And I asked, "What are catacombs?" He responded, "They were hiding places, where the first Christians had to hide when there were persecutions, and sometimes they were killed in these places." This phrase impressed me, and I cherished it in my soul. When he said this to me and my siblings, it impressed me with a feeling of admiration for people who are killed because of their faith. For me, as a boy, it was very sublime and noble. This discovery of the existence of the catacombs greatly impressed me throughout my childhood.

3

Gertrude Detzel (1903-1971)

ANOTHER EXAMPLE FROM the time of the martyrs and confessors that impressed me very much was the saintly virgin and Servant of God Gertrude Detzel (1903–1971), who died as a confessor of the Faith on August 16, 1971, in Karaganda, the diocese where I arrived in 1999 and where I served as an auxiliary bishop from 2006 to 2011.

One of the reasons why the Catholic faith in the Soviet Union did not die but, on the contrary, was alive and active, was the presence of many devout, deeply religious, courageous women who loved God, who kept the Faith, and passed it on to subsequent generations. Gertrude Detzel was one of these courageous confessors. God gave her a special calling to serve the persecuted Church; she became a real organizer of church life among the numerous exiled Catholics in Kazakhstan. The heroic example of her life is still a fresh memory, since many faithful of my previous diocese were educated by this holy virgin during their childhood and youth. Under the constant threat of being arrested, she intrepidly exercised her calling as a catechist, traveling and visiting Catholic families secretly, catechizing not only children but also adult persons during the night. In dangerous situations, she even baptized children, in times and places where there were no priests available. During such circumstances of prolonged absence of priests, she led prayers during burials and when a Catholic couple, in the presence of witnesses, celebrated their wedding. (The Code of Canon Law says that marriages are validly celebrated before witnesses alone if it is foreseen that the absence of the person competent to assist at the celebration of marriage [usually the parish priest] will persist for a month.)

Camps and prisons could not crush Gertrude's fervor in professing the Faith. Despite being under the strict supervision of the special Communist commandant's office, she secretly held prayer meetings at home and services on Sundays, as there were no priests due to many of them being imprisoned or under house arrest. Though she risked being sentenced to twenty years of hard labor for leaving the special settlement without authorization, Gertrude nevertheless, together with her sister Valentina, secretly visited the surrounding villages inhabited by Catholics (especially Germans deported from the Wolga and Black Sea regions). She walked dozens of miles on foot, baptizing children and adults, teaching people to pray, copying out prayers. Gertrude became the first catechist for many future priests and nuns. She was a "Eucharistic woman" with a priestly soul. She had a deep veneration for priests and for their sacred ministry and was happy to obey them and be submitted in obedience to their pastoral guidance. In her house, Bl. Oleksiy Zaritskiy often celebrated Holy Mass secretly. People saw something special in her: she was always focused on God, praying for a long time on her knees. Gertrude told the faithful, "Pray, and you will have a priest!"

Gertrude spent several years in a labor camp. The situation of many women in the labor camp was aggravated by the anxiety of having children at home, abandoned to the mercy of fate, with no one to care for them. Gertrude constantly consoled the mothers overwhelmed by these thoughts: "God will help. God laid this cross on us and will help us bear it." When, finally, "from above" they gave permission to bring the children to their mothers in the labor camp, Gertrude became their teacher, taught them to pray and sing. Those who were born in the labor camp needed baptism, those who died needed a funeral service. Gertrude did both. Under her leadership, an altar was erected in the women's barracks, and the Catholics observed all religious holidays.

On Sundays, women gathered in the barracks for general prayer, and rumors about this, of course, reached the camp authorities. One day, during Sunday prayers, the commandant appeared in the barracks. Fearing the worst, all the women were filled with fright, and only Gertrude continued to read the prayer in a calm and even voice. Having finished praying and rising from her knees, she approached the commandant: "I beg your pardon, we are Catholics; when we pray, we talk to God and therefore cannot be interrupted." To these words, the commandant, a Kazakh by nationality, only nodded understandingly and patted Gertrude on the shoulder. (Among Kazakh Muslims, disturbing a person during prayer has always been considered a sign of ignorance and bad manners.) "Everything is clear to me," he replied. "Your faith is correct. If you had stopped praying and had run away, I wouldn't have believed you. Continue praying." With these words, he left the barracks.

Gertrude was arrested by the Communist authorities, being accused of "anti-revolutionary religious propaganda," and was sentenced to ten years in concentration camps. During her imprisonment in the camps of forced labor and in prisons, Gertrude Detzel managed to organize groups of catechism and prayer among the prisoners. Even during the tormenting nightly KGB interrogations, she tried to catechize her jailers. Often, in the middle of the night, Gertrude was woken up by the prison guard: "Detzel, to the boss!" Throwing on humid outer garments (as she had no spare clothes, during the night her outerwear needed to dry), Gertrude unquestioningly followed the guards, but as soon as she entered the office of the head of the prison, she was the first to initiate conversation from the threshold: "Mr. Chief, today is such and such a holiday" (depending on the time: the Ascension of the Lord, the Descent of the Holy Spirit, the Dormition of the Blessed Virgin Mary, etc.). Then Gertrude briefly outlined the corresponding Gospel event and concluded, "This is a time of grace, and on such a holiday you are disturbing a woman at night because of some nonsense." Unable to object to anything, the boss, closing his eyes, began to brush her off and called on the guards, "Take her away, take her back, she has bewitched me; I too am already beginning to believe!"

The Communist authorities liberated her from the prison to prevent the entire prison from turning into a kind of underground church. At her final release from prison, the prison authorities read aloud the list of her "crimes": "she was catechizing people, she was baptizing, she buried the dead, she visited the sick, she organized groups of prayer." After hearing of such "crimes," one of the jailers was moved and said frankly, "We have before us a saintly woman!" After the decree of release was read to her, Gertrude first thanked God ("For all good things come from God"), then the authorities and everyone present. Then she spoke these memorable words to them: "I am a Catholic. Our faith requires us to pass on all our knowledge to our neighbor and help him; for whatever you do for your neighbor, you do for God." Saying goodbye to Gertrude, all members of the court rose and, wishing her a good journey, shook her hand.

On the day of her funeral, Gertrude Detzel, who had always been accustomed to being content with little in life, lay covered in flowers, and there seemed to be no end to the flow of children, youth, and adults who came to say goodbye to her. "She lay there like an angel," recalled the people, in a sky-blue blouse and with a gentle smile on her face. The people could not help wishing to gaze upon her ceaselessly.

On August 15, 2021, on the eve of the fiftieth anniversary of the death of the Servant of God Gertrude Detzel, the diocesan stage of the process of her beatification was opened by the bishop of Karaganda in the basilica of St. Joseph.

Part III

Eminent Examples of Martyrdom

1

The Blessed Virgin Mary

THE BLESSED VIRGIN stood at the foot of the Cross of her Divine Son, the redeemer of mankind. According to St. Ildephonsus, "the sufferings of Mary exceeded those of all martyrs united together." Hence, she is called the "Queen of martyrs." Even though she did not die physically at the foot of the Cross, nevertheless we can say that she has suffered more than all other creatures combined.

The great theologian Fr. Réginald Garrigou-Lagrange said that the most profound cause by which the Blessed Virgin Mary was motivated in bearing her pains at Calvary was the intensity of her love of God, of her Son, and of souls. The very root of these her sufferings, as of those of Jesus, was the sins of humankind. The saints suffer from sin in proportion to their love of God and of their neighbor (see *The Mother of the Saviour and Our Interior Life*, part 1, chap. 3, art. 5). This coredemptive love of Mary surpassed the most ardent charity of the great saints, that of Saint

Peter, Saint Paul, and Saint John. In her, the initial fullness of charity already exceeded the final grace of all the saints put together. Fr. Réginald Garrigou-Lagrange says,

> The cause of her sufferings was the sum total of all the sins put together, of all the revolts, of all the sacrilegious anger brought in an instant to their paroxysm in the sin of deicide, in the relentless hatred against Our Lord. To form a lively idea of the sufferings of Mary, one would have to have received, like the stigmatized, the impression of the wounds of the Saviour; it would be necessary to have participated in all his physical and moral sufferings, by the crucifying graces which make the way of the cross relive the most painful hours of the Passion of Christ. On the Calvary of the Heart of Jesus grace and charity overflow in the heart of his holy Mother; it is he who strengthens her, as she herself sustains Saint John spiritually. Jesus offers his martyrdom to her, and she offers herself with this Son who is much dearer to her than her own life. (see *The Mother of the Saviour and Our Interior Life*, part 1, chap. 3, art. 5)

St. Bernard of Clairvaux explained how Our Lady suffered more than all the martyrs, saying,

> Truly, O blessed Mother, a sword has pierced your heart. For only by passing through your heart could the sword enter the flesh of your Son. Indeed, after

> your Jesus—who belongs to everyone, but is especially yours—gave up his life, the cruel spear, which was not withheld from his lifeless body, tore open his side. Clearly it did not touch his soul and could not harm him, but it did pierce your heart. For surely his soul was no longer there, but yours could not be torn away. Thus, the violence of sorrow has cut through your heart, and we rightly call you more than martyr, since the effect of compassion in you has gone beyond the endurance of physical suffering. (*Sermo in dominicam infra octavam Assumptionis* 14)

St. Alphonsus of Liguori said, "Mary was the Queen of Martyrs, for her martyrdom was longer and greater than that of all the Martyrs. . . . As Jesus is called the King of sorrows and the King of martyrs, because He suffered during His life more than all other martyrs, so also is Mary with reason called the Queen of martyrs, having merited this title by suffering the most cruel martyrdom possible after that of her Son" (*The Glories of Mary*, discourse 9). In the Vespers Hymn for the Feast of the Seven Dolors, the Church salutes her, singing, "The Virgin stands there the while, more noble than the martyrs. By a new wonder, O Mary, dying, thou dost not die, though transfixed by such great and dreadful sorrows."

In virtue of her Immaculate Conception, the body of the Blessed Virgin Mary was exempt from physical macerations and wounds. She was also free from bodily sicknesses. The death of Our Lady was not from a sickness or physical disintegration, which are the result of original sin, but from love and her longing to see her Beloved Son in heaven. The suffering of Our Lady, properly speaking, was the suffering in her spirit, in her heart and soul, which were pierced by the sword, as the Prophet Simeon had foretold (see Luke 2:35). Her deepest suffering was a spiritual one, because of the unspeakable evil of sin, which offends God. The Catechism of the Council of Trent teaches us, "As the Conception of Our Lord itself transcends the order of nature, so also His birth. . . . Just as the rays of the sun penetrate without breaking or injuring in the least the solid substance of glass, so after a like but more exalted manner did Jesus Christ come forth from his mother's womb without injury to her maternal virginity" (part 1, chap. 4.7). The Church thus prays in the Preface of the Mass of the Blessed Virgin Mary at the Foot of the Cross: "The Virgin Mary, who without pain had given birth to the divine Son, suffered unspeakable pains for our regeneration."

The type of the sufferings endured by the Blessed Virgin Mary was that of compassion and love. The Benedictine Abbot Arnold of Chartres (+1160) spoke of a double altar on Calvary: "One in the Heart of Mary, the other in the Body of Christ. Christ sacrificed His flesh, Mary her soul"

(*De septem verbis Domini in cruce* 3). St. Alphonsus, quoting Saint Antoninus, says:

> While other martyrs suffered by sacrificing their own lives, the Blessed Virgin suffered by sacrificing her Son's life, a life that she loved far more than her own; so that she not only suffered in her soul all that her Son endured in His body, but moreover the sight of her Son's torments brought more grief to her heart than if she had endured them all in her own person. No one can doubt that Mary suffered in her heart all the outrages which she saw inflicted on her beloved Jesus. Anyone can understand that the sufferings of children are also those of their mothers who witness them. . . . Also did Mary suffer all those torments, scourges, thorns, nails, and the cross, which tortured the innocent flesh of Jesus, all entered at the same time into the heart of this Blessed Virgin, to complete her martyrdom. "He suffered in the flesh, and she in her heart," writes Blessed Amadeus. "So much so," says Saint Lawrence Justinian, "that the heart of Mary became, as it were, a mirror of the Passion of the Son, in which might be seen, faithfully reflected, the spitting, the blows and wounds, and all that Jesus suffered." Saint Bonaventure also remarks that "those wounds—which were scattered over the body of our Lord—were all united in the single heart of Mary." (*The Glories of Mary*, discourse 9)

Fr. Réginald Garrigou-Lagrange gives us a deep explanation of how Mary's spiritual pains continued each time she participated at the Holy Mass, celebrated by the Apostle John:

> Holy Mass was for her, to a degree we can only suspect, the memorial and the continuation of the sacrifice of the Cross. A sword of sorrow had pierced her heart on Calvary, the strength and tenderness of her love for Jesus making her suffer a true martyrdom. She suffered so much that the memory of Calvary could never grow dim, and each Holy Mass was a fresh renewal of all that she had lived through there. Mary found the same Victim on the altar when John said Mass. She found the same Jesus, really present; not present in image only, but in the substance of His Body with His Soul and Divinity. True, there was no immolation in blood, but there was a sacramental immolation, realised through the separate consecration of the bread and the wine: Jesus' blood is shed sacramentally on the altar. How expressive is that figure of His death for her who cannot forget, for her who bears always in the depths of her soul the image of her Son, outraged, and wounded, for her who hears yet the insults and the blasphemies offered Him. St. John's Mass, with Mary present at it, was the most striking memorial of the Cross as it is perpetuated in its substance on our altars. (*Mother of the Saviour*, part 1, chap. 3, art. 5)

St. Alphonsus of Liguori, in his book *The Glories of Mary*, quotes St. Bonaventure, who interrogates the Sorrowful Mother with these words: "Oh Lady, where art thou? Near the cross? Nay, on the cross, thou art crucified with thy Son" (*On the Fifth Dolor of the Death of Jesus*). In the same book, St. Alphonsus explains the correct theological meaning of the coredemptive work of Mary, saying, "Indeed, the death of Jesus was more than enough to save the world, and an infinity of worlds; but this good Mother, for the love she bore us, wished also to help the cause of our salvation with the merits of her sufferings, which she offered for us on Calvary. Therefore, Blessed Albert the Great says, 'that as we are under great obligations to Jesus for His Passion endured for our love, so also are we under great obligations to Mary, for the martyrdom which she voluntarily suffered for our salvation in the death of her Son'" (discourse 9).

Pope Pius X presents the traditional Catholic teaching on the redemptive value of the sufferings of Mary at the foot of the Cross:

> It was not only the prerogative of the Most Holy Mother to have furnished the material of His flesh to the Only Son of God, Who was to be born with human members, of which material should be prepared the Victim for the salvation of men; but hers was also the office of tending and nourishing that Victim, and at the appointed time presenting Him for the sacrifice. Hence

> that uninterrupted community of life and labors of the Son and the Mother, so that of both might have been uttered the words of the Psalmist, "My life is consumed in sorrow and my years in groans" (Ps. 30:11). (*Ad diem illum* [February 2, 1904], 12)

Fr. Réginald Garrigou-Lagrange explains that the two mysteries of the Incarnation and the Redemption do not constitute a duality that would diminish the unity of Christology, since they are united in the redemptive Incarnation (see *Mother of the Saviour*, part 1, chap. 3, art. 5), and he continues to explain, "In her capacity as Mother of God the Redeemer, she was indeed united to him by a perfect conformity of will, by humility, poverty, suffering, tears, above all at Calvary; in this sense she satisfied with him, and this satisfaction of convenience derives its very great value from her eminent dignity as Mother of God, from the perfection of her charity, from the fact that she had nothing to expiate for herself, and from the intensity of her suffering" (*Mother of the Saviour*, part 2, chap. 2, art. 3). And Pope Benedict XV teaches, "By uniting herself to the Passion and death of her Son, she suffered as if to die . . . to appease divine justice; as much as she could, she immolated her Son, in such a way that one can say that with him she redeemed the human race" (*Inter Sodalicia* [March 22, 1918]). Since the word *Co-Redemptrix* signifies of itself simple cooperation in the work of redemption, and since it has received in the theological usage of centuries the very precise meaning of secondary and dependent cooperation, there can be no serious objection to its use, on condition that it be accompanied by some expression indicating that Mary's role in this cooperation is secondary and dependent (see Réginald Garrigou-Lagrange, *Mother of the Saviour*, part 2, chap. 2, art. 3).

The liturgical and devotional tradition of the Church gave us in the Sequence *Stabat Mater* a spiritual masterpiece of a meditation on the sorrowful Virgin Mary, a poignant meditation on Mary's pain at the foot of the Cross. The devotion to Our Lady of Sorrows found its artistic representation especially in the Pietà, depicting the Virgin Mary cradling the dead body of Jesus after His body was removed from the Cross. In moments of harsh suffering, when we feel abandoned and alone, we must remind ourselves that we have a loving Mother, who has a maternal and compassionate heart that endured the greatest pains a creature could ever endure here on earth. St. Gabriel of the Sorrowful Virgin Mary wrote in one of his letters, "The loving Virgin of Sorrows who cannot see our miseries without compassionating them, will keep us safe enough under her protecting mantle, and she employs for our defence those same swords which have pierced her blessed and spotless heart. Let us compassionate Mary's sorrows and she herself will infallibly compassionate ours. Oh, what sweetness and calm one feels when one throws oneself on her maternal protection! If Mary is for us, who shall be against us?" (Letter to his father, 9 September 1861).

The Sorrowful Mother helps us to accept and carry the crosses of our whole lives, and those of every day, without rebelling, but with love and faith. She bends over us when we are in pain, sadness, and abandonment. She teaches us to make our life an offering to God for the conversion of sinners and the spread of the Catholic faith. Fr. Frederick William Faber (+1863) left us the following inspiring reflections about the great spiritual advantage we may acquire through devotion to Our Sorrowful Mother:

> We can never help thinking of sin, so long as we see those seven swords, springing, like a dreadful sheaf, from the very inmost sanctuary of her broken heart. Yet there is something also in the dolors, and even in this abhorrence of sin, to make us forget ourselves, without at all periling our safe humility. We rise up from the contemplation of them with a yearning for the conversion of sinners. . . . The house of sorrow is always a house of love. This is what takes place in us regarding Mary's dolors. One of the thousand ends of the Incarnation was God's condescending to meet and gratify the weakness of humanity, for ever falling into idolatry because it was so hard to be always looking upwards, always gazing fixedly into inaccessible furnaces of light. So are Mary's

dolors to her grandeurs. The new strength of faith and devotion, which we have gained in contemplating her celestial splendours, furnishes us with new capabilities of loving; and all our loves, the new and the old as well, rally round her in her agony at the foot of the Cross of Jesus. Love for her grows quickest there. It is our birthplace. We became her children there. She suffered all that because of us. Sinlessness is not common to our Mother and to us. But sorrow is. It is the one thing we share, the one common thing betwixt us. We will sit with her therefore, and sorrow with her, and grow more full of love, not forgetting her grandeurs,—Oh surely never!—but pressing to our hearts with fondest predilection the memory of her exceeding martyrdom. . . . It is a beautiful and a dread sight, to see all the sorrows of fallen earth resumed in the broken heart of our own Mother. Has it moved us? Then why not for the rest of life, in sober panic at the world and worldliness, go and sit at our Mother's feet and meditate her griefs? Is there a fitter work for prodigals come back to their Heavenly Father? Compassion with her is already compassion with Jesus; and we may say that compassion with the Invisible Creator Himself is the devotional feeling out of which we shall serve Him most generously, and realize Him most tenderly as our Eternal Father,—eternal because He has been, blessed be His Majesty from all eternity, and eternal because we shall be, blessed be His compassion!, with Him, His happy sons, His pardoned sons, to all eternity. Truly Mary lays us evermore in the lap of God. Truly by some celestial logic of their own, all Christian things, be they doctrines or devotions, come out at last in that one compendious, melodious, alone-sufficing word, Eternal Father! (*The Foot of the Cross, or The Sorrows of Mary* [London: 1858], pp. 72; 74–75; 492)

2
The Maccabean Martyrs

In the traditional Roman Rite, August 1st is the feast of the Seven Maccabee Brothers, long celebrated as a commemoration on the feast of St. Peter's Chains. Their martyrdom is narrated in the seventh chapter of the Second Book of the Maccabees. The feast of the Maccabees was kept as part of the feast of St. Peter's Chains, since the same Roman basilica that houses the chains also keeps, directly underneath them in a crypt under the altar, the relics of these saints. Many Church Fathers preached sermons on the seven Maccabees, including St. Cyprian of Carthage, St. Ambrose of Milan, St. Gregory of Nazianzus, and St. John Chrysostom.

In a homily, St. Gregory of Nazianzus commends Eleazar as "the first-fruits of those who suffered in this world before Christ . . . (who) offered seven sons, the fruits of his discipline, a living sacrifice, holy, pleasing to God, more splendid and pure than every sacrifice of the Law; for it is most right and just to refer to the father what belongs to the sons." The liturgical texts of the Byzantine Rite, on the other hand, refer to Eleazar several times not as their father, but as their teacher. This seems to have been inferred from the last verse of 2 Maccabees 6: "Thus did this man die, leaving not only to young men, but also to the whole nation, the memory of his death for an example of virtue and fortitude," since his death is followed immediately by the heroic martyrdom of the seven young men.

St. Gregory of Nazianzus defended the Maccabean martyrs against those who opposed their veneration, arguing that they were not Christians. He presents the Maccabean heroes, namely the elderly priest Eleazar, who is praised as the first pre-Christian martyr, and the seven youths with their mother, praised for their heroic steadfastness (see *Or. 20 In Macchabaeos* 5–6). Especially admirable is the brave reply of the children to King Antiochus, by which they refuse to abandon their ancestral traditions and betray God and the Mosaic Law, and instead declare their willingness to die (see *In Macchabaeos* 7–8). They accept their fate with an enthusiasm that astonishes everyone. Their mother witnesses their martyrdom, cheering and encouraging them (see *In Macchabaeos* 9–10). Once they have died, she rejoices over the triumph of her children and rushes willingly into the fire to die as a martyr herself (see *In Macchabaeos* 11–12). The story of the Maccabees must be held in the same esteem as that of Daniel and the three Hebrew Youths (see Dan. 3; 6), and of all the Christian martyrs. It provides models for priests, mothers, and children, who should imitate the heroes of this story.

St. Gregory of Nazianzus explains thus the meaning of the Church's liturgical veneration of the Maccabean martyrs:

> But why the Maccabees? This festival is indeed theirs, even though they are not honoured by many, because their martyrdom was not after Christ. Yet they deserve to be honoured by everyone, because they suffered for the sake of their ancestral traditions. For what else would they have done, those who suffered martyrdom before Christ's passion, if they had been persecuted after the time of Christ, and had been able to emulate His death on our behalf? Indeed, these men displayed valour of this magnitude without the benefit of such a model: how then could they not have gained in heroic stature, had they undertaken their trial with the example before them? This is a somewhat mystic and arcane thing to say, but at the same time very persuasive, at least for me and for all those who love God: none of those consummated before the coming of Christ attained their end without faith in Christ. For the Logos was later openly proclaimed in His own era, but He was made known even before to the pure of mind, as is evident from the large number of persons who obtained honour before His day. Such figures, then, are not to

> be overlooked because they lived before the time of the cross but should rather be acclaimed for having lived in accordance with the cross and are entitled to the honour that words bestow. (*In Macchabaeos* 1–2)

Already St. Ignatius of Antioch, a disciple of the apostles, wrote, "The holy prophets lived according to Christ Jesus. On this account were they also persecuted, who by his grace were inspired, to the end that the disobedient might be fully persuaded that there is one God who manifested himself through Jesus Christ, his Son, who is his eternal Word" (*Magn*. 8.2).

St. John Chrysostom answers the objection "that the Maccabees didn't shed their blood for Christ, but for the law and the edicts that were in the law, in that they were killed over pig's flesh" (*Eleaz. puer*. 4) by explaining the true identity of the giver of the Old and the New Covenants, as attested by the prophet Jeremiah (see Jer. 31:31–34). He uses Jeremiah's words to make his argument that Christ had presented both the new and the old covenants (see *Eleaz. puer*. 7), thus proving that it was "Christ [who] gave the law," that the "people who were killed for the law" must therefore have "shed their blood for the giver of the law" (*Eleaz. puer*. 16).

St. Augustine responded to the Jewish claims of ownership of the Maccabees by defending the Maccabees as martyrs of Christ (martyres Christi), and by affirming, "Some

Jew steps forward and says to us, 'How can you reckon these people of ours to be your martyrs? How can you be so unwise as to celebrate their memory? Read their confessions; see whether they confessed Christ'" (*Mart. Mach.* 300.3). St. Augustine claims that the practice of dying for the Mosaic law, which actually entailed dying for "Christ veiled in the law," did not differ in any significant way from the practice of dying for "Christ unveiled in the Gospel. Only a Jew could not see this, their eyes still being veiled" (see 2 Cor. 3:14–16) (*Mart. Mach.* 300.5).

The Preface of the feast of the Maccabean Martyrs in the Ambrosian Rite presents a theological synthesis of their liturgical veneration by the Church:

> Truly it is worthy and just, meet and profitable to salvation, that we, o Lord, in honour of Thy name, in the yearly feast of Thy Holy Martyrs the Maccabees, should celebrate with all wonderment those who, being brothers by birth, were companions in martyrdom. Their glorious mother conceived them in body and in spirit, so that those whom she had borne into this world according to the flesh, she might also beget for glory unto almighty God, in spiritual fecundity. For those who were born according to the flesh that they might die, died piously unto life. Their tongues were cut out, their scalps taken, but amid these things, these most glorious youths did not grieve for the cruelty of their

torments, but exulted that they died all the more gloriously, that they might each be a comfort and example to the others. After the rest, their mother by both blood and faith followed them at last, not that she might be last, but that before herself she might send to God the fruits of her womb, and so in peace follow her beloved sons. What then can we say, and with what exultation, for the fact that on the day of their passion, there passed from this world to the seat of eternity the witness of the faith and confessor of the truth Eusebius? who on that very day, on which the martyrs of the Old Law suffered, as a champion of the New Testament was also taken to heaven. The former departed observing the commandments of the Jewish law; the latter fell asleep, affirming the unity of the undivided Trinity. Through Christ our Lord etc.

3

The Innocent Martyrs of Bethlehem

The feast of the Holy Innocents has been celebrated liturgically by the Church since the fifth century. These infants are venerated as martyrs, though they died not only for Christ but actually instead of Christ. St. Augustine called them the Church's first blossoms, killed by the frost of persecution the moment they showed themselves. He further explained the deep spiritual meaning of the martyrdom of the Innocents:

> Blessed are you, Bethlehem in the land of Judah! You suffered the inhumanity of King Herod in the murder of your babes, and thereby have become worthy to offer to the Lord a pure host of infants. In full right do we celebrate the heavenly birthday of these children whom the world caused to be born unto an eternally blessed life rather than that from their mothers' womb, for they attained the grace of everlasting life before the enjoy-

> ment of the present. The precious death of any martyr deserves high praise because of his heroic confession; the death of these children is precious in the sight of God because of the beatitude they gained so quickly. For already at the beginning of their lives they pass on. The end of the present life is for them the beginning of glory. These then, whom Herod's cruelty tore as sucklings from their mothers' bosom, are justly hailed as "infant martyr flowers"—they were the Church's first blossoms, matured by the frost of persecution during the cold winter of unbelief. (*Sermo 10 de Sanctis*)

St. Quodvultdeus (+450), Bishop of Carthage, said, "Even before they learn to speak, they proclaim Christ. The children die for Christ, though they do not know it. The parents mourn for the death of martyrs. The child makes of those as yet unable to speak fit witnesses to himself. See the kind of kingdom that is his, coming as he did in order to be this kind of king. See how the deliverer is already working deliverance, the Savior already working salvation" (*Sermon on the Feast of the Holy Innocents*).

St. Bernard of Clairvaux thus explained the true martyrdom of the Holy Innocents:

> Who has any doubt that the Holy Innocents have received the martyr's crown? He who does not admit this, who does not admit that the crown of martyrdom has been the reward of the infants slain for Christ, ought

also to disbelieve that infants regenerated in Christ are numbered amongst the children of adoption. For how could that Little One Who was born not against us but for us, have suffered so many other little ones of His own time to be slaughtered on His account, when with the will He might have prevented it, unless He had prepared for them something more precious than the life they were robbed of? We may then suppose that the martyrdom they endured for Christ's sake was sufficient to sanctify them, just as circumcision sufficed for the salvation of other infants at that time, and as baptism suffices now, without any voluntary co-operation. And if you ask what their merit before God was that they should be crowned, inquire also what was their crime against Herod that they should be slain. Shall the mercy and love of Christ, think you, be outdone by Herod's wickedness, so that He shall not have power to crown the infants done to death for His sake? . . . But the Innocents were truly and in a special sense Thy martyrs, O Lord, because the power and excellence of Thy grace Thou hast clearly manifested in them, in whom neither men nor angels could discover any merit. Thus, as the Psalmist predicted, "out of the mouth of infants and sucklings Thou hast perfected praise." "Glory to God in the highest," sang the angels, "and on earth peace to men of good will." That, my brethren, was great praise, indeed: but I make bold to affirm, it was as yet imperfect, until the coming of Him Who should say, "Suffer the lit-

> tle children and forbid them not to come to Me, for the kingdom of heaven is for such," and until there should be peace for men in the sacrament of mercy even without the co-operation of their own will. Let those who are fond of disputing so contentiously about the intention and the act weigh these things well. Let them observe and consider that neither must be neglected even when both are not in our power; especially because, where we cannot have the two, either without the other may suffice, not only for salvation, but even for sanctification. But let them be firmly persuaded of this also, that although the act without the intention may be enough for salvation, the act against the intention profits nothing; so that the very same thing—the mere external act—which for the infant merits a crown, becomes for the hypocrite a cause of damnation. Furthermore, the intention is sometimes sufficient without the act, yet not against the act. (*Sermon for the Feast of the Holy Innocents*)

Regarding the efficacy of circumcision, one can distinguish two aspects in circumcision. So far as it was a rite of the Mosaic Law, it did not communicate grace; but it did confer grace insofar as it was an external profession of faith in the Redeemer to come; just as the blood of the Paschal lamb saved the Jews from the destroying angel, not because it was the blood of a lamb but because it typified the Blood of Christ (see St. Thomas, *ST*, III, q. 62, a. 6 c; also *In Ep. ad Rom.*, c. 4, lect. 2).

4

St. John the Baptist

We can consider St. John the Baptist as a precursor not just of every person who "prophetically" preaches the truth but specifically of every person who consciously preaches the truth of Jesus Christ at the cost of his own life. The word of God in John 1:7 characterized the life and mission of St. John the Baptist as a witness: "This man came for a witness" (*eis martyrian*). The witness of the Lord's precursor consisted concretely in giving witness to the incarnated Word of God, Who is the only true light in the world (see John 1:8–9). The authentic preaching and suffering for the sake of the truth must refer to Jesus Christ, the Incarnate God, and to the truth of the Catholic faith in general. St. Bede the Venerable gave a concise explanation of the martyrdom of St. John the Baptist as a witness of Christ, Who is the Truth:

> There is no doubt that blessed John suffered imprisonment and chains as a witness to our Redeemer, whose forerunner he was, and gave his life for him. His perse-

cutor had demanded not that he should deny Christ, but only that he should keep silent about the truth. Nevertheless, he died for Christ. Does Christ not say: I am the truth? Therefore, because John shed his blood for the truth, he surely died for Christ. Through his birth, preaching and baptizing, he bore witness to the coming birth, preaching and baptism of Christ, and by his own suffering he showed that Christ also would suffer. Such was the quality and strength of the man who accepted the end of this present life by shedding his blood after the long imprisonment. He preached the freedom of heavenly peace yet was thrown into irons by ungodly men; he was locked away in the darkness of prison, though he came bearing witness to the Light of life and deserved to be called a bright and shining lamp by that Light itself, which is Christ (see John 5:35). John was baptized in his own blood, though he had been privileged to baptize the Redeemer of the world, to hear the voice of the Father above him, and to see the grace of the Holy Spirit descending upon him. But to endure temporal agonies for the sake of the truth was not a heavy burden for such men as John; rather it was easily borne and even desirable, for he knew eternal joy would be his reward. Since death was ever near at hand through the inescapable necessity of nature, such men considered it a blessing to embrace it and thus gain the reward of eternal life by acknowledging Christ's name. Hence the apostle Paul rightly says: You have been

> granted the privilege not only to believe in Christ but also to suffer for his sake. (*Hom.* 23)

St. Thomas Aquinas rightly explains the meaning of true martyrdom and that of St. John the Baptist:

> Martyrs are so called as being witnesses, because by suffering in body unto death they bear witness to the truth; not indeed to any truth, but to the truth which is in accordance with godliness, and was made known to us by Christ: wherefore Christ's martyrs are His witnesses. Now this truth is the truth of faith. Wherefore the cause of all martyrdom is the truth of faith.
>
> But the truth of faith includes not only inward belief, but also outward profession, which is expressed not only by words, whereby one confesses the faith, but also by deeds, whereby a person shows that he has faith, according to James 2:18, "I will show thee, by works, my faith." Hence, it is written of certain people (Titus 1:16): "They profess that they know God but in their works they deny Him." Thus, all virtuous deeds, inasmuch as they are referred to God, are professions of the faith whereby we come to know that God requires these works of us, and rewards us for them: and in this way they can be the cause of martyrdom. For this reason, the Church celebrates the martyrdom of Blessed John the Baptist, who suffered death, not for refusing to deny the faith, but for reproving adultery. (*ST*, II–II, q. 124, a. 5 c)

5

St. Stephen

St. Stephen is venerated as the protomartyr, or first martyr, of Christianity. He was one of the first seven deacons whom the apostles ordained (see Acts 6:5–6). St. Stephen is not only a martyr; he is one of the most striking personages of the apostolic age, so much so that, as the Greek Church gives him the title of apostle, so the Traditional Roman Liturgy places him in the category of the prophets, wise men, and scribes whose cruel fate is described in the Gospel of his feast (see Matt. 23:34–39). St. Stephen prayed to God to forgive his murderers.

> The prayer of Stephen was heard, and its wondrous answer was Paul. The piety of the early Pontiffs led them to emphasize this connection between the protomartyr and the Apostle by building, about the sixth century, beside the tomb of St. Paul in the Via Ostiensis, a notable oratory, with a monastery attached to it, in honour of St. Stephen. In an age of such enfeebled energy, of

> so many compromises with conscience, of such regard for human respect and opinion, what an example of Christian fortitude is given us by Stephen when, confronting the Sanhedrim, he declares to the Jewish people the most unpalatable truths. (Ildefonso Schuster, *Sacramentary (Liber Sacramentorum): Historical and Liturgical Notes on the Roman Missal* [London: 1924], p. 381)

St. Augustine presents St. Stephen as the first imitator of the example of Christ:

> Christ, the Head of Martyrs, also suffered for us, leaving us an example, that you should follow his steps. And the steps of the Passion of this same Head of Martyrs did blessed Stephen follow close, in that he was stoned by the Jews for his confession of Christ, and thereby gained the crown which pertained to him in virtue of his name. For in the Greek language the word Stephen does signify a crown. Thus, he already bore the name crown, whereby was foretold the palm of martyrdom, which same he was to gain when he was stoned to death. Yet notwithstanding, he sought not to draw down vengeance on his persecutors, but contrariwise prayed God to forgive them. (*Sermo 2 de S. Stephano*)

On the martyrdom of St. Stephen, St. Fulgentius, Bishop of Ruspe (+533), pronounced the following luminous sermon:

> Yesterday we celebrated the birth in time of our eternal King. Today we celebrate the triumphant suffering of his soldier. Yesterday our king, clothed in his robe of flesh, left his place in the Virgin's womb, and graciously visited the world. Today his soldier leaves the tabernacle of his body and goes triumphantly to heaven. Our king, despite his exalted majesty, came in humility for our sake; yet he did not come empty-handed. He brought his soldiers a great gift that not only enriched them but also made them unconquerable in battle, for it was the gift of love, which was to bring men to share in his divinity. He gave of his bounty, yet without any loss to himself. In a marvellous way he changed into wealth the poverty of his faithful followers while remaining in full possession of his own inexhaustible riches. And so, the love that brought Christ from heaven to earth raised Stephen from earth to heaven; shown first in the king, it later shone forth in his soldier. Love was Stephen's weapon by which he gained every battle, and so won the crown signified by his name. His love of God kept him from yielding to the ferocious mob; his love for his neighbour made him pray for those who were stoning him. Love inspired him to reprove those who erred, to make them amend; love led him to pray for those who

stoned him, to save them from punishment. Strengthened by the power of his love, he overcame the raging cruelty of Saul and won his persecutor on earth as his companion in heaven. In his holy and tireless love, he longed to gain by prayer those whom he could not convert by admonition. (*Sermo* 3.1–3)

6
St. Peter

Tradition tells us that St. Peter was crucified upside down at Vatican Hill. He felt unworthy to be martyred exactly as Our Lord. What is the significance of St. Peter's martyrdom for the Church, especially his being crucified upside down? Divine Providence decreed that the first pope should die not only as a martyr but a death of crucifixion, in order for this death to approach even exteriorly to the death of Our Lord on the Cross. Yet, St. Peter died, according to the tradition, being crucified upside down. This detail of his death should be an eloquent sign that the papal office should be marked by the virtue of humility as its outstanding characteristic. The Primacy of the Bishops of Rome, or the Papal Primacy, is the highest spiritual power in the militant Church of Christ on earth. The dogma of Faith teaches this to us: "If anyone says that the Roman pontiff has merely an office of supervision and guidance, and not the full and supreme power of jurisdiction over the whole church, and this not only in matters of faith and morals, but also in those which concern the discipline and government of the church dispersed throughout the whole world; or that he has only the principal part, but not the absolute fullness, of this supreme power; or that this power of his is not ordinary and immediate both over all and each of the churches and over all and each of the pastors and faithful: let him be anathema" (I Vatican Council, *Pastor Aeternus*, chap. 3, canon). While possessing the supreme jurisdictional power, the pope must keep in mind that his power is only a vicarious power, since he is only the Vicar of Christ and only participates in the power of Christ, Who is the Divine Shepherd and Head of the Church. Pope St. Gregory the Great (+604) was the pope who extensively adopted the significant title "servant of the servants of God" (servus servorum Dei). He wrote, "Through the burden of being a shepherd, I have become the servant of all" (*Ep.* 11.26).

St. Gregory the Great stressed the use of this papal title as an answer to John the Faster, the bishop of Constantinople, who usurped the title of "Ecumenical Patriarch." In the *Life of St. Gregory*, we read, "He refuted the name 'universal' and first of all began to write himself 'servant of the servants of God' at the beginning of his letters, with sufficient humility, leaving to all his successors this hereditary evidence of his meekness" (John the Deacon, *Vita S.*

Gregorii 2.1). The example of the first Pope, St. Peter, in dying crucified upside down, should remain for every pope a salutary warning. The pope is actually the one who has the least freedom in the Church, since he is bound by the Divine deposit of Faith and the example of the humility of St. Peter and other great popes.

After Our Lord asks St. Peter three times whether he loves Him, Our Lord said to St. Peter, "Amen, amen I say to thee, when thou wast younger, thou didst gird thyself, and didst walk where thou wouldst. But when thou shalt be old, thou shalt stretch forth thy hands, and another shall gird thee, and lead thee whither thou wouldst not" (John 21:18). These words of Our Lord to His Vicar on earth mean that the fundamental attitude of a pope must be the readiness to suffer for the sake of uncompromising fidelity to the main task that the Lord entrusted to him; that is, to keep untainted and unchanged the integrity of the deposit of the Revealed Faith, as Christ said, "I have prayed for thee, that thy faith fail not: and thou, being once converted, confirm thy brethren" (Luke 22:32).

We possess several heroic examples of popes who preferred death, injuries, and exile rather than betray the Catholic faith or even to yield to compromises or ambiguities regarding the Catholic truth. Pope St. Martin I (+655) was the last pope who died a martyr. Yet he died not at the hands of pagan persecutors who would have asked him to worship idols, as was the case with all the martyr popes until the Emperor Constantine, but as a victim of the persecution of a heretical Christian emperor. Pope Martin I firmly resisted the heresy of Monothelitism (that holds that Christ has only one will). In the following lines from a letter of Pope St. Martin I, we can grasp the heroic attitude that every pope should have in unambiguously keeping and defending the integrity of the Catholic faith:

> God wishes all men to be saved and to come to a knowledge of the truth through the prayers of Peter. Hence, I pray that God will strengthen their hearts in the orthodox faith, help them to stand firm against every heretic and enemy of the Church, and guard them unshaken. And this I ask especially for their shepherd, now designated to be over them, that none may fall or go astray or renounce anything, however trifling, which they professed in writing in the sight of the Lord and his holy angels. In this way, together with me in my humiliation, they will receive the crown of justice in the true faith from the hand of our Lord and Savior Jesus Christ. For the Lord himself will take care of this lowly body of mine as befits his providence, whether this means unending suffering or some small consolation. Why am I anxious? The Lord is near. But my hope is in his compassion that he will not delay in putting an end to this course which he has assigned to me. (*Ep*. 17)

Another luminous example of a pope as a confessor of the Faith is St. Nicholas I, the Great (+867), who went down in history as a defender of marriage. King Lothair II of Lotharingia (+869) wanted to divorce his legitimate wife and marry his mistress. He bribed a papal legate and the bishops of a synod in Metz in 863 to approve the annulment of his marriage. After careful examination, Pope Nicholas I condemned the false annulment and deposed the bishops who had consented to it. Thereupon King Lothair II marched his armies to Rome and cornered the pope in St. Peter's basilica, demanding that the pope recognize the annulment. Pope Nicholas I was ready to die rather than to yield to an invalid marriage annulment. Despite having no food and being threatened with severe personal injuries for several days, Pope Nicholas I remained unshakably firm as a defender of the indissolubility of marriage.

Another example of extraordinary courage in defending the rights of the Church against the usurpation of spiritual powers by a secular authority was Pope St. Gregory VII (+1085) during the "Investiture Controversy," when Holy Roman Emperor Henry IV (1054–1105) claimed to perform the investiture of bishops. St. Gregory VII was ready to die rather than to make a compromise on that matter. His noble Apostolic courage is expressed in the following words:

> Such are the anxieties to which we are prey, that even those who live with us, not only can no longer suffer them, but cannot even bear the sight of them. For us, very often life is a boredom and death an ardent wish. If it happens that Jesus, the tender comforter, true God and true man, deigns to stretch out his hand to me, his goodness restores joy to my afflicted heart; but as soon as he withdraws, my trouble becomes excessive. As for me, I am constantly dying; as for him I live at times. If my strength completely fails, I cry out to him, I say to him in a groaning voice: "If you imposed such a heavy burden on Moses and Peter, they would, it seems to me, be overwhelmed. What can become of me who am nothing compared to them? You have therefore, Lord, only one thing to do: it is to govern yourself, with your Peter, the pontificate which is imposed on me; otherwise, you will see me succumb, and the pontificate will be covered with confusion in my person." (Letter to Abbot Hugh of Cluny, 7 May 1078)

He died in exile, and his last words were a rephrasing of a verse from Psalm 44: "I have loved justice and hated iniquity, and so I die in exile."

7

St. Paul

St. Paul was also martyred not too far from the place of St. Peter's martyrdom. Tradition holds that he was beheaded. Is there not a profound meaning in the Church's celebrating these two saints' feast day together on June 29? The two apostles Peter and Paul are indeed the apostles who exercised the greatest influence at the beginning of the Church. St. Peter was the first pope and vicar of Christ on earth, and St. Paul was the apostle who "laboured more abundantly than all" the other apostles (1 Cor. 15:10), being called the greatest missionary of the Church of all times, the teacher of the gentiles (see 1 Tim. 2:7), and according to the liturgical tradition of the Church, the "teacher of the world" (magister mundi). Since the first centuries, both apostles were called the two founding pillars of the Church in Rome. The old Christian hymn *Decora lux aeternitatis* (*Vespers hymn of the feast of St. Peter and St. Paul*) praises the two apostles as the "parents of Rome." The oldest testimony of the common martyrdom of the apostles Peter and Paul in Rome is given by St. Clement (+96), a disciple of the apostles and the third pope after St. Peter. He wrote,

> Let us take the noble examples furnished in our own generation. Through envy and jealousy the greatest and most righteous pillars of the Church have been persecuted and put to death. Let us set before our eyes the illustrious apostles. Peter, through unrighteous envy, endured not one or two, but numerous labours, and when he had finally suffered martyrdom, departed to the place of glory due to him. Owing to envy, Paul also obtained the reward of patient endurance, after being seven times thrown into captivity, compelled to flee, and stoned. After preaching both in the east and west, he gained the illustrious reputation due to his faith, having taught righteousness to the whole world, and come to the extreme limit of the west, and suffered martyrdom under the prefects. Thus, was he removed from the world, and went into the holy place, having proved himself a striking example of patience. (*1 Clem.* 5)

St. Irenaeus of Lyons (+200), a disciple of St. Polycarp, who, in turn, was a disciple of the apostle St. John, witnessed about the Church of Rome, which he calls "the very great, the very ancient, and universally known Church founded and organized at Rome by the two most glorious apostles, Peter and Paul" (*Adv. Haer.* 3.3.2). We possess a splendid sermon of Pope St. Leo the Great (+461) on the common, inseparable contribution of these two apostles in founding the Roman church, showing thereby its primacy in the entire Christian world:

> Rome is the place where the chief of the Apostles met their glorious end. For these are the men, through whom the light of Christ's gospel shone on you, O Rome, and through whom you, who were the teacher of error, were made the disciple of Truth. These are your holy Fathers and true shepherds, who gave you claims to be numbered among the heavenly kingdoms, and built you under much better and happier auspices than they, by whose zeal the first foundations of your walls were laid: and of whom the one that gave you your name defiled you with his brother's blood. These are they who promoted you to such glory, that being made a holy nation, a chosen people, a priestly and royal state (see 1 Ptr. 2:9), and the head of the world through the blessed Peter's holy See you attained a wider sway by the worship of God than by earthly government. (*Sermo* 82.1)

St. Paul was present at the martyrdom of the first martyr, St. Stephen. So, in effect, St. Stephen witnessed to St. Paul. The first and extraordinary great fruit of the martyrdom of St. Stephen was the conversion of Saul, who became an apostle of Christ, the teacher of the gentiles, and the greatest missionary of the Church. St. Augustine said,

As for the man who was still Saul, for whom it was not enough for Stephen to have been killed . . . he received letters from the priests and scribes, so that wherever he might find men of this way, that is Christians, he should bring them back bound to face the sort of punishment Stephen had received. And off went Saul in his wrath, off went the wolf to the sheepfolds, to the flocks of the Lord; like a rabid wolf he was thirsting for blood, breathing out slaughter, off he went on the road. And Christ from above: Saul, Saul, why are you persecuting me? (see Acts 9:1–4). Wolf, wolf, why are you persecuting the Lamb? I, when I was killed, slew the lion. Why are you persecuting me? Rid yourself of the wolf; from wolf become sheep, from sheep become shepherd. The beauty of the picture which shows the stoning of Stephen and the conversion of Saul together. This man is Paul, an apostle of Christ Jesus (see 1 Cor. 1:1), this man is Paul, the servant of Christ Jesus (see Rom. 1:1). Yes, you listened very well to the voice saying: Why are you persecuting me? (see Acts 9:4). You were laid low, you were raised up; laid low as a persecutor, raised up as a preacher. Tell us, let us hear it: Paul, the servant of Christ Jesus by the will of God (see 2 Cor. 1:1). Certainly not by your will, was it, dear Saul? We know, we have seen your fruits that came by your will; Stephen was slain by your will. We can see your fruits that came by the will of God: you are read everywhere, chanted everywhere, everywhere you are converting to Christ the hearts that oppose him, everywhere as a good shepherd you are gathering huge flocks. You are reigning with the one you stoned, reigning with Christ. There you can both see each other; can both now hear my sermon; both of you please pray for us. He will listen to you both, the one who crowned you, one first, the other later on, one who suffered persecution, the other who did the persecuting. The first was a lamb then, the other was a wolf; now, though, both are lambs. (*Sermo* 316.4–5)

8
The Apostles

EVERY APOSTLE EXCEPT St. John the Evangelist was martyred. There is a message that tells us that those who are closest to Our Lord will inevitably suffer the most. St. John the Evangelist, indeed, did not die a martyr's death. Yet, a very old tradition of the Church says that he was brought to Rome in order to be martyred through a very cruel death, namely, by being thrown into a cauldron of boiling oil. Divine Providence, however, did not want his death and saved him miraculously. At least since the eighth century, the Roman Church commemorated this miracle with a proper feast on May 6, called "St. John the Apostle before the Latin Gate" (Sancti Ioannis Apostoli ante portam Latinam). Despite the fact that the Roman Church had been celebrating this feast for twelve hundred years, Pope John XXIII removed it from the liturgical calendar in 1960. Tertullian, a writer from the end of the second and beginning of the third century, wrote that at Rome, the Apostle John was put into a vessel of boiling oil, but he came out cleaner and healthier than he went in (see *De praescript.* 36).

St. John the Evangelist continuously carried in his soul the readiness to shed his blood for his beloved Master, Jesus Christ. He was longing for martyrdom, also bearing in mind that all his colleagues, the apostles, gave the supreme witness to Christ in dying a martyr's death. St. Jerome (+420) explains this spirit of martyrdom that St. John the Evangelist nurtured in his soul:

> The question arises how the sons of Zebedee, namely, James and John, drank the cup of martyrdom, since Scripture tells only that James the Apostle was beheaded by Herod, but John died a natural death. But if we read the history of the Church, in which it is told that he also for the sake of his witness (to Christ) was cast into a vessel of boiling oil, and thence went forth as a champion of Christ to receive his crown, and was at once exiled to the island of Patmos, we see that his spirit did not fail at the prospect of martyrdom, and that John did drink the cup of confession that the three children in the fiery furnace also drank, although the persecutor did not shed their blood. (*In Matt.* 3.20)

It is true that those who are closest to the Lord participate more deeply in the mystery of His passion. God Himself gave us an example in suffering in His human nature out of love for us sinners, as we read in the Holy Scripture:

"God so loved the world, as to give his only begotten Son" (John 3:16), and: "[God] spared not even his own Son, but delivered him up for us all" (Rom. 8:32). Through His loving suffering, Jesus Christ brought His human nature to perfection: "It became him, for whom are all things, and by whom are all things, who had brought many children into glory, to perfect the author of their salvation, by his passion" (Heb. 2:10).

A perfect disciple of Christ is he who is in the closest manner united with Christ's sufferings and interiorly conformed to His death, as St. Paul teaches: "That I may know him, and the power of his resurrection, and the fellowship of his sufferings, being made conformable to his death" (Phil. 3:10). For St. Ignatius, the martyr bishop of Antioch (+107) and a disciple of the apostles, to be a perfect Christian signifies to imitate Christ in His passion. Deeply moving are these his words: "Then I shall truly be a disciple of Jesus Christ when the world will not even see my body. Pray to Christ for me that by these means I may be found a sacrifice of God. . . . May I benefit from the wild beasts prepared for me, . . . Now I begin to be a disciple" (*Rom.* 4–5).

We possess some deep insights from St. Therese of the Child Jesus, where she explains that the closer we are to God, the more we share in the mystery of suffering, which is love, in order to save souls: "I shall not fear God's strikes, for, even in the most bitter sufferings, I always feel that it is His gentle hand that is striking. I desire only one thing when I shall be in Carmel, and it is to suffer always for Jesus. Life passes so quickly that really it must be better to have a very beautiful crown and a little trouble than to have an ordinary one without any trouble. And then for a suffering borne with joy, when I think that during the whole of eternity, I will love God better. Then in suffering we can save souls" (Letter to Sr. Agnes (Pauline), 18 March 1888). In the poem "Living on Love," which St. Therese wrote in February 1895, she says, "Dying of Love is a truly sweet martyrdom, and that is the one I wish to suffer." St. Therese succinctly formulated the fundamental law of the Christian life in these words: "We must go to heaven by the same way, that of suffering united to love" (Letter to Abbé Maurice Bellière, 18 July 1897). Suffering has a salvific purpose, as St. Therese so dramatically expressed it in some of her last words: "Never would I have believed it was possible to suffer so much! Never! Never! I cannot explain this except by the ardent desires I have had to save souls" (*Last Conversations* [September 30, 1897]).

In the Gospel, we hear the famous account of St. James the Greater and St. John the Evangelist's mother imprudently asking Our Lord for her sons to sit on His right and left in Heaven. Our Lord reminded them, "My chalice indeed you shall drink; but to sit on my right or left hand, is not mine to give to you, but to them for whom it is prepared by my Father" (Matt. 20:23). St. James the Greater is believed to have been the first apostle to have been martyred: "And at the same time, Herod the king stretched forth his hands, to afflict some of the church. And he killed James, the brother of John, with the sword" (Acts 12:1). So, James the Greater did in fact drink the chalice.

Most certainly, martyrdom is firstly a gift of God, a grace that conforms a Christian interiorly and also exteriorly in a most perfect way to Jesus Christ. The Lord gave us the example and invites those to imitate Him whom He in His Divine wisdom has chosen to follow Him through martyrdom. The Apostles James and John had at first a too earthly view of Christ's glory. The Lord said to them, "Can you drink the chalice that I shall drink? They say to him: We can." Then He replied to them, "My chalice indeed you shall drink; but to sit on my right or left hand, is not mine to give to you, but to them for whom it is prepared by my Father" (Matt. 20:22–23). St. John Chrysostom gave us the following explanation:

> After that [the Lord] adds, 'Are ye able to drink of the cup that I shall drink of, and to be baptized with the baptism that I am baptized with?' Do you see, how He straightway drew them off from their suspicion, by framing His discourse from the contrary topics? For you, He says, talk to me of honor and crowns, but I to you of conflicts and labors. For this is not the season for

> rewards, neither shall that glory of mine appear now, but the present time is one of slaughter, and wars, and dangers. And see how by the form of His question, He both urges and attracts them. For He said not, "Are ye able to be slain?" "Are ye able to pour forth your blood?" But how? "Are ye able to drink of the cup?" Then to attract them to it, He says, "which I shall drink of," that by their fellowship with Him in it they might be made more ready. And a baptism again calls He it; showing that great was the cleansing the world was to have from the things that were being done. "They say unto Him, We are able." Out of their forwardness they straightway undertook it, not knowing even this which they were saying, but looking to hear what they had asked. What then says He? "You shall drink indeed of my cup, and be baptized with the baptism that I am baptized with." Great blessings did He foretell to them. His meaning is, you shall be counted worthy of martyrdom, and shall suffer these things which I suffer; you shall close your life by a violent death, and in these things you shall be partakers with me. (*In Matt.* 20.2)

Martyrdom, both a spiritual and physical one, is without a doubt a real suffering and a cross that one must bear. Yet, such a suffering and a cross are a special grace that the eternal love of God has prepared and chosen for that concrete person.

9

St. Ignatius of Antioch (+107)

St. Ignatius, surnamed *Theophorus* or God-bearer, was a disciple of St. John the Evangelist. According to some early Christian writers, the apostles St. Peter and St. Paul directed that he should succeed St. Evodius (+70) as bishop of Antioch, an office that he retained for forty years, proving himself in every way an exemplary pastor of souls. Alban Butler writes,

> From an early period it was believed that Trajan cross-questioned the soldier of Christ in such terms as these: "Who are you, spirit of evil, who dare to disobey my orders and who goad others on to their destruction?" "No one calls Theophorus spirit of evil," the saint is said to have replied. "Who is Theophorus?" "He who bears Christ within him." "And do not we bear within ourselves those gods who help us against our enemies?" asked the emperor. "You are mistaken when you call gods those who are no better than devils," retorted Ignatius. "For there is only one God who made heaven

and earth and all that is in them: and one Jesus Christ into whose kingdom I earnestly desire to be admitted." Trajan inquired, "Do you mean Him who was crucified under Pontius Pilate?" "Yes, the same who by His death has crucified both sin and its author and has proclaimed that every malice of the devil should be trodden under foot by those who bear Him in their hearts." "Do you then carry about Christ within you?" said the emperor. Ignatius answered, "Yes, for it is written, 'I will dwell in them and will walk with them.'" When Trajan gave sentence that the bishop should be bound and taken to Rome to be devoured by the wild beasts for the entertainment of the people, the saint exclaimed, "I thank thee, O Lord, for putting within my reach this pledge of perfect love for thee, and for allowing me to be bound for thy sake with chains, after the example of thy apostle Paul." The voyage appears to have been a very cruel ordeal, for Ignatius was guarded night and day by ten soldiers who were so brutal that he says they were like "ten leopards" and he adds that he was "fighting with wild beasts on land and sea, by day and night" and "they only grow worse when they are kindly treated." At Smyrna, he had the joy of meeting his former fellow disciple St Polycarp, and hither also came Bishop Onesimus at the head of a deputation from Ephesus, Bishop Damas with envoys from Magnesia, and Bishop Polybius from Tralles. (*Butler's Lives of the Saints*, ed. Herbert J. Thurston and Donald Attwater [London: 1956], 1:219–220)

> In the letter to Tralles, Ignatius tells that community to keep from heresy, "which you will do if you remain united to God, even Jesus Christ, and the bishop and the ordinances of the apostles. He who is within the altar is clean, but he that is outside it, that is, who acts independently of the bishop, priests and deacons, is not clean." The fourth letter, addressed to the Christians in Rome, is an entreaty to them to do nothing to prevent him from winning the crown of martyrdom; there was, he thought, some danger that the more influential would try to obtain a mitigation of his sentence. His alarm was not ill-founded. Christianity at this date had made converts in high places. Such men as Flavius Clemens, the cousin of the emperor, and the Acilii Glabriones had powerful friends in the administration. The pagan satirist Lucian (c. 165 A.D.), who almost certainly was familiar with these letters of Ignatius, bears witness to the same effect. (*Butler's Lives of the Saints*, 1:220)

His ardent desire to achieve a most perfect union with Christ through martyrdom was expressed by St. Ignatius in these words of his *Letter to the Romans*, which are considered as one of the most beautiful witnesses of a Catholic spirituality of martyrdom:

> I shall never have another such opportunity of attaining unto my Lord. . . . Therefore you cannot do me a greater

favour than to suffer me to be poured out as a libation to God whilst the altar is ready; that, forming a choir in love, you may give thanks to the Father by Jesus Christ that God has vouchsafed to bring me, a Syrian bishop, from the east to the west to pass out of this world, that I may rise again unto Him.

. . . Only pray for me that God may give me grace within as well as without, not only to say it but to desire it, that I may not only be called but be found a Christian. . . .

. . . Suffer me to be the food of wild beasts through whom I may attain unto God. I am God's grain, and I am to be ground by the teeth of wild beasts that I may be found the pure bread of Christ. Rather entice the beasts to become my sepulchre, that they may leave nothing of my body, that when I am dead, I may not be troublesome to any man. . . . I do not command you, as Peter and Paul did: they were apostles, whereas I am a culprit under sentence: they were free, but I am even yet a slave. But if I suffer, I shall then become the freedman of Jesus Christ and in Him I shall arise free. . . .

. . . I have joy of the beasts that are prepared for me, and I heartily wish that they may devour me promptly: nay, I would even entice them to devour me immediately and wholly, and not to serve me as they have served some whom they have been afraid to touch. If they are unwilling to meddle with me, I will even compel them. Excuse me in this matter. I know what is good for me.

> Now I begin to be a disciple. May nothing visible or invisible begrudge me that I may attain unto Jesus Christ. Come fire and cross, gashes and rendings, breaking of bones and mangling of limbs, the shattering in pieces of my whole body; come all the wicked torments of the devil upon me if I may but attain unto Jesus Christ.
>
> All the pleasures of the world, and all the kingdoms of this earth, shall profit me nothing. It is better for me to die on behalf of Jesus Christ, than to reign over all the ends of the earth. "For what shall a man be profited, if he gains the whole world, but lose his own soul?" Him I seek, who died for us: Him I desire, who rose again for our sake. This is the gain which is laid up for me. Pardon me, brethren: do not hinder me from living, do not wish to keep me in a state of death; and while I desire to belong to God, do not give me over to the world. Allow me to obtain pure light: when I have gone there, I shall indeed be a perfect man. Permit me to be an imitator of the passion of my God. If anyone has Him within himself, let him consider what I desire, and let him have compassion with me, as knowing how I am straitened. (*Rom.* 2.2, 3.1, 4.1–3, 5.2–3, 6.1–3)

St. Ignatius sees his martyrdom as an act similar to the Eucharistic sacrifice. He therefore speaks of the "sacrificial altar" (*thysiastērion*) at which he wants to be offered (see *Rom.* 2.2). In several places in his letters (cf. *Eph.* 5.2; *Magn.* 7.2; *Trall.* 7.2; *Phd.* 4), he describes the altar at which the Eucharistic sacrifice is celebrated, the "sacrificial altar" (*thysiastērion*). In his *Letter to the Philadelphians*, St. Ignatius highlights the importance of the union of the Church through the celebration of the Eucharistic sacrifice: "Use one Eucharist; for the flesh of the Lord Jesus Christ is one and the cup is one, to unite us all in His blood. There is one altar, as there is one bishop, together with the body of the priesthood and the deacons, my fellow servants, that whatever you do, you may do according to God" (*Phd.* 4).

> St Ignatius of Antioch is the first writer outside the New Testament to lay stress upon the virgin-birth. To the Ephesians, for example, he writes, "And from the prince of this world were hidden Mary's virginity and her child-bearing, in like manner also the death of the Lord" (*Eph.* 19.1). The mystery of the Trinity, too, is plainly taken for granted, and we detect a definite approach to clear Christological conceptions when we read in the same letter (chap. 7), "There is one Physician, of flesh and of spirit, begotten and unbegotten, God in man, true Life in death, son of Mary and son of God, first passible and then impassible, Jesus Christ our Lord." Not less remarkable are the phrases used in connection with the Holy Eucharist. It is "the flesh of Christ," "the gift of God," "the medicine of immortality," and Ignatius denounces the heretics "who confess not that the Eucharist is the flesh of our Saviour Jesus

Christ, which flesh suffered for our sins and which in His loving-kindness the Father raised up." Finally, it is in the letter to the Smyrnaeans that for the first time in Christian literature we find mention of "the Catholic Church." "Wherever," he writes, "the bishop appears, there let the people be, even as wherever Christ Jesus is, there is the Catholic Church" (*Sm.* 8.2). The saint often speaks severely of the heretical speculations—in particular, those of the docetists—which already in his day were threatening harm to the integrity of the Christian faith. It might indeed be said that the keynote of all his instruction was insistence upon unity of belief and spirit among those who professed to be our Lord's followers. But, with all his dread of heresy, he emphasizes the need of indulgence towards the erring and urges patient forbearance and the love of the cross. The exhortation he addresses to the Ephesians provides a lesson for everyone whose religion is no empty name: "And for the rest of men pray unceasingly —for there is in them hope of repentance—that they may attain unto God. Suffer them therefore to be instructed by the example of your works. In face of their outbursts of wrath be meek; in face of their boastful words be humble; meet their revilings with prayers; where they are in error be steadfast in the faith; in face of their fury be gentle. Be not eager to retaliate upon them. Let our forbearance prove us their brethren. Let us endeavour to be imitators of the Lord, striving who can suffer the greater wrong, who can be defrauded, who be set at naught, that no rank weed of the Devil be found in you. But in all purity and sobriety abide in Christ Jesus in flesh and in spirit" (*Eph.* 10.1–3). (*Butler's Lives of the Saints*, 1:223)

Part IV

The Fatima Message and Martyrdom

1

The Fatima Message and Martyrdom

The third secret was revealed by the Blessed Virgin Mary to the children at the Cova in Fatima on July 13, 1917. It was to be kept in the greatest confidence. When Sister Lucia was with the Dorothean Sisters in Tuy, Spain, she fell ill in mid-1943. Because it was feared that she might die before the third secret was revealed by her, the bishop of Leiria requested that she write down the remainder of the secret (or third secret) told to the children in 1917. Obediently, Sister Lucia wrote it down on a single sheet of paper. She placed it in an envelope and sealed it.

This is the text of Sister Lucia, which was made public on May 13, 2000, at the beatification Mass of Francisco and Jacinta Marto in Fatima:

J.M.J.

The third part of the secret revealed at the Cova da Iria-Fatima, on 13 July 1917.

I write in obedience to you, my God, who command me to do so through his Excellency the bishop of Leiria and through your Most Holy Mother and mine.

After the two parts which I have already explained, at the left of Our Lady and a little above, we saw an Angel with a flaming sword in his left hand; flashing, it gave out flames that looked as though they would set the world on fire; but they died out in contact with the splendour that Our Lady radiated towards him from her right hand: pointing to the earth with his right hand, the angel cried out in a loud voice: "Penance, Penance, Penance!" And we saw in an immense light that is God: "something similar to how people appear in a mirror when they pass in front of it," a Bishop dressed in White: "we had the impression that it was the Holy Father." Other Bishops, Priests, men and women Religious going up a steep mountain, at the top of which there was a big Cross of rough-hewn trunks as of a cork-tree with the bark; before reaching there the Holy Father passed through a big city half in ruins and half trembling with halting step, afflicted with pain and sorrow, he prayed for the souls of the corpses he met on his way; having reached the top of the mountain, on

> his knees at the foot of the big Cross he was killed by a group of soldiers who fired bullets and arrows at him, and in the same way there died one after another the other Bishops, Priests, men and women Religious, and various lay people of different ranks and positions. Beneath the two arms of the Cross there were two Angels each with a crystal aspersorium in his hand, in which they gathered up the blood of the Martyrs and with it sprinkled the souls that were making their way to God. (Tuy-3-1-1944)

Sister Lucia also confirmed this published text. She met with Bishop Seraphim de Sousa of Leiria at her Carmelite convent in Coimbra, Portugal, on April 27, 2000. Two envelopes were presented to her by the bishop. The first envelope was the outer envelope containing the second envelope, which held the third secret. Sister Lucia touched the letter and stated, "This is my letter." She then read it and said, "This is my writing." She was asked if it was the only third secret. She said, "Yes, this is the third secret, and I never wrote another."

The third part of the secret of Fatima describes a great martyrdom that will include the martyrdom of the pope as well as of many other bishops, priests, religious, and laypersons. This great martyrdom is seen in the future. From the "Theological Commentary on the Message of Fatima" of the Congregation for the Doctrine of the Faith, we read,

> In the vision we can recognize the last century as a century of martyrs, a century of suffering and persecution for the Church, a century of World Wars and the many local wars which filled the last fifty years and have inflicted unprecedented forms of cruelty. In the "mirror" of this vision we see passing before us the witnesses of the faith decade by decade. Here it would be appropriate to mention a phrase from the letter which Sister Lucia wrote to the Holy Father on 12 May 1982: "The third part of the 'secret' refers to Our Lady's words: 'If not, [Russia] will spread her errors throughout the world, causing wars and persecutions of the Church. The good will be martyred; the Holy Father will have much to suffer; various nations will be annihilated.'"

Yet, one must see the dramatic scenes of persecution and martyrdom in the supernatural view of Christian faith and hope. The "Theological Commentary on the Message of Fatima" emphasizes the value of martyrdom for the spiritual renewal of the life of the Church:

> It is a consoling vision, which seeks to open a history of blood and tears to the healing power of God. Beneath the arms of the cross angels gather up the blood of the martyrs, and with it they give life to the souls making their way to God. Here, the blood of Christ and the blood of the martyrs are considered as one: the blood of the martyrs runs down from the arms of the

cross. The martyrs die in communion with the Passion of Christ, and their death becomes one with his. For the sake of the body of Christ, they complete what is still lacking in his afflictions (see Col. 1:24). Their life has itself become a Eucharist, part of the mystery of the grain of wheat which in dying yields abundant fruit. The blood of the martyrs is the seed of Christians, said Tertullian. As from Christ's death, from his wounded side, the Church was born, so the death of the witnesses is fruitful for the future life of the Church. Therefore, the vision of the third part of the "secret," so distressing at first, concludes with an image of hope: no suffering is in vain, and it is a suffering Church, a Church of martyrs, which becomes a sign-post for man in his search for God. The loving arms of God welcome not only those who suffer like Lazarus, who found great solace there and mysteriously represents Christ, who wished to become for us the poor Lazarus. There is something more: from the suffering of the witnesses there comes a purifying and renewing power, because their suffering is the actualization of the suffering of Christ himself and a communication in the here and now of its saving effect. (Issued as part of the document *The Message of Fatima* by the Congregation in May 2000)

Conclusion

THE CATHOLIC FAITH—the integral and pure Catholic faith—is the greatest treasure, which God put in our soul at the moment of our baptism. And for the sake of this Faith, a Catholic must be ready, with God's grace, to give his life. A Catholic is marked with the Cross of Christ since his baptism and must manifest the mystery of Christ's Cross in all his life, even, if necessary, through martyrdom. Immediately before we were baptized, we heard this question: "What do you ask from the Church?" (Quid petis ab Ecclesia?), and the godparents answered in our name, or when we were adults, we answered ourselves only this one and decisive word: "Faith" (fidem). This "faith" meant the integral and pure Catholic faith. The next question was: "What does faith give you?" The answer was again most short, decisive, and unsurpassable: "Eternal life (vitam aeternam)."

Saint Fidelis, who was martyred by Protestants because of his uncompromising fidelity to the Catholic faith, gave his last sermon a few days before he shed his blood to bear witness to his preaching. These are the words he left as a testament:

> O Catholic faith, how solid, how strong you are! How deeply rooted, how firmly founded on a solid rock! Heaven and earth will pass away, but you can never pass away. From the beginning the whole world opposed you, but you mightily triumphed over everything. This is the victory that overcomes the world, our faith. It has subjected powerful kings to the rule of Christ; it has bound nations to his service. What made the holy apostles and martyrs endure fierce agony and bitter torments, except faith? What is it that today makes true followers of Christ cast luxuries aside, leave pleasures behind, and endure difficulties and pain? It is living faith that expresses itself through love. It is this that makes us put aside the goods of the present in the hope of future goods. It is because of faith that we exchange the present for the future.

May the following prayer help all Catholics to remain always aware of the importance of confessing the Faith and being a witness of Christ. St. Polycarp (+155) recited the following prayer immediately before the pyre was lit on which he consummated his martyrdom as an offering and a sacrifice to God for a scent of sweetness (see Eph. 5:2), in imitation of our Lord Jesus Christ, "the faithful witness, (*martys pistos*)" (Apoc. 1:5):

Lord, almighty God, Father of your beloved and blessed Son Jesus Christ, through whom we have come to the knowledge of yourself, God of angels, of powers, of all creation, of all the race of saints who live in your sight, I bless you for judging me worthy of this day, this hour, so that in the company of the martyrs I may share the cup of Christ, your anointed one, and so rise again to eternal life in soul and body, immortal through the power of the Holy Spirit. May I be received among the martyrs in your presence today as a rich and pleasing sacrifice. God of truth, stranger to falsehood, you have prepared this and revealed it to me and now you have fulfilled your promise. I praise you for all things, I bless you, I glorify you through the eternal priest of heaven, Jesus Christ, your beloved Son. Through him be glory to you, together with him and the Holy Spirit, now and for ever. Amen.